200 fab fish dishes

hamlyn | all colour cookbook

200 fab fish dishes

Gee Charman

An Hachette UK Company
www.hachette.co.uk

First published in Great Britain in 2009 by Hamlyn,
a division of Octopus Publishing Group Ltd
2–4 Heron Quays, London E14 4JP
www.octopusbooks.co.uk

ISBN: 978-0-600-61932-1

A CIP catalogue record for this book is available from the
British Library

Printed and bound in China

1 2 3 4 5 6 7 8 9 10

Both metric and imperial measurements have been given
in all recipes. Use one set of measurements only, and not
a mixture of both.

Standard level spoon measurements are used in all recipes.
1 tablespoon = one 15 ml spoon
1 teaspoon = one 5 ml spoon

Ovens should be preheated to the specified temperature
– if using a fan-assisted oven, follow the manufacturer's
instructions for adjusting the time and the temperature.

Fresh herbs should be used unless otherwise stated.

Medium eggs should be used unless otherwise stated.

The Department of Health advises that eggs should not be
consumed raw. This book contains some dishes made with
raw or lightly cooked eggs. It is prudent for vulnerable people
such as pregnant and nursing mothers, invalids, the elderly,
babies and young children to avoid uncooked or lightly cooked
dishes made with eggs. Once prepared, these dishes should
be kept refrigerated and used promptly.

This book includes dishes made with nuts and nut
derivatives. It is advisable for those with known allergic
reactions to nuts and nut derivatives and those who may be
potentially vulnerable to these allergies, such as pregnant and
nursing mothers, invalids, the elderly, babies and children, to
avoid dishes made with nuts and nut oils. It is also prudent to
check the labels of pre-prepared ingredients for the possible
inclusion of nut derivatives.

contents

introduction

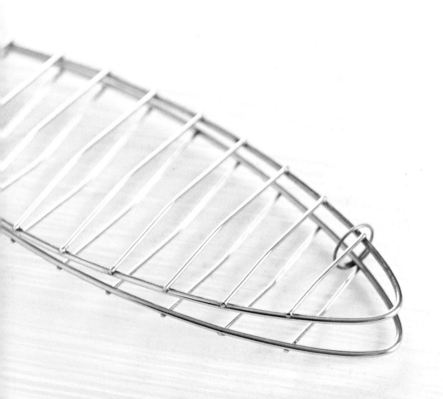

introduction

Fish is the original fast food. It is quick to prepare and cook, and with so many different types of fish and shellfish on the market you could eat a different type every night for over a month.

The fish used in the recipes of this book can easily be changed for other types of fish. The general rule is to try and get the same type of fish if the one stated is not your favourite or is unavailable. White-fleshed, round fish, such as sea bass, can be replaced by red or grey mullet. Instead of flat fish, such as plaice, you can use bream, Dover sole or lemon sole. King prawns can be changed for tiger prawns, cockles for mussels or clams and salmon for trout or sea trout.

Most of the recipes are quick to prepare and cook, although some require a little advanced planning for marinating or slow cooking. However, the actual amount of time you will be in the kitchen is never that long and the results will be delicious.

There are six chapters in the book – nibbles, soups and stews, salads and starters, pastas, pulses and grains, main courses and barbecue – and the quantities in many of these recipes can be changed to make the nibbles a starter or the starters a main course, for example. The barbecue recipes could also be adapted for less-good weather by using a grill, an oven or a really hot frying pan.

Buying fish and shellfish

There are a few key points that should be followed when buying fish and shellfish. In all cases, always buy it fresh, as the fresher the fish the better the flavour and texture. It is easiest to tell how fresh whole fish are by looking at them. Whole fish should have bright, clear eyes, ruby-red gills, a clear slime covering the fish and, most importantly, they should not smell 'fishy'. Fresh fish smells of the sea and not of fish!

With fish that has already been filleted, it is a little more difficult to judge how fresh it is, but the flesh should be firm and the skin bright, and it should smell of the sea.

The freshness of shellfish is very important, so always ask your fishmonger when it was caught. It should be no more than a day old, or two at the very most. Again, there should be no strong smell of fish.

Mussels, clams and cockles should be bought and cooked live. Many supermarkets sell these types of shellfish in vacuum-sealed packets, which suffocate them. These should be avoided if at all possible.

Ethical sourcing of fish

For many years the seas around the world have been overfished, with different species being affected at different times as popularity fluctuates with fashions and trends. Unfortunately, the consequence of

FOR RECIPES USING	YOU COULD ALSO TRY...
ANCHOVIES	Sprats • Sardines • Whitebait
CLAMS	Mussels • Oysters • Cockles • Razor Clams
COD	Pollack • Hoki • Haddock • Coley • Hake • Whiting (large)
CRAYFISH	Langoustines • Prawns (large)
HADDOCK, SMOKED	Kippers • Smoked Cod
HAKE	Cod
HALIBUT	Brill • Turbot
HERRINGS	Mackerel • Pilchards • Sardines
MACKEREL	Sardines • Herrings • Pilchards
MACKEREL, SMOKED	Smoked Eel • Smoked Salmon • Smoked Trout
MONKFISH	Cod
PERCH	Salmon • Trout
PLAICE	Dover Sole • Lemon Sole • Dab (large) • Flounder
PRAWNS	Scallops • Langoustine (Dublin Bay Prawns) • Scampi
RED MULLET	Tilapia • Sea Bream • Sea Bass
RED SNAPPER	Sea Bream • Red Mullet • Red Bream • Grey Mullet
SALMON	Trout • Salmon Trout • Sea Trout
SARDINES	Herrings • Pilchards • Mackerel (small)
SEA BASS	John Dory • Turbot • Brill
SEA BREAM	Red Bream • Red Mullet • Red Snapper • Grey Mullet
SQUID (CALAMARI, INKFISH)	Cuttlefish • Octopus
SWORDFISH	Ray • Shark • Tuna
TROUT, SMOKED	Smoked Mackerel • Smoked Eel
TUNA	Shark • Swordfish • Bonito • Mahi Mahi
TURBOT	Halibut • Brill

overfishing still affects the world's waters today. New laws are now in place in most countries to try to prevent this from happening again and to allow diminished stocks to recover. In addition, careless fishing, in which unwanted sea creatures are caught in the fishing nets often to die in the water, or are hauled up on to the decks only to be tossed back into the sea as waste, is having an impact on fish stocks, as well as being cruel. Make sure, therefore, that you always buy dolphin-friendly tuna.

It is now vital that consumers take matters into their own hands and check that the fish they are buying is ethically and sustainably sourced. If you don't know where the fish you are buying has come from, then don't buy it. There are so many alternatives (see chart, opposite) and good-quality farmed fish is now so widely available, that we can easily allow our natural stock to replenish. There are many web sites that will tell you which fish are endangered in certain waters from around the world and which species are safe to buy, making it easier to buy ethically.

Farmed fish is obviously an ethical way of sourcing certain types of fish, but it has had a bad press over the years due to the overcrowding of sea cages, especially in the case of salmon farming. If you are buying farmed fish, try to buy organic, as the cages tend to be less densely stocked and no chemicals are used, which is better for our health. Look for government recognition on the packets of farmed fish to ensure high standards of husbandry.

Storing fish

Fish should be kept for only 1–2 days in the refrigerator. The refrigerator temperature should be between 1°C (34°F) and 5°C (41°F). Fish should be removed from any packaging and placed on a clean plate, covered with a clean, damp cloth and then loosely covered with clingfilm. The same method should be used for scallops and prawns.

Mussels, clams and cockles are difficult to keep alive, as they are easily suffocated. The best way, if you are storing the shellfish overnight, is to place them in a colander with a few ice cubes or ice flakes set over a bowl in the refrigerator. Keep topping up the ice as it melts.

Fresh fish can be frozen, although freezing does change the flavour and texture a little. If you want to freeze your own fish, make sure you buy it as fresh as possible. Wrap it up in clingfilm and place it in a sealable plastic bag or airtight container (which will reduce the likelihood of freezer burn), then place it in the freezer.

Allow frozen fish to thaw out in the refrigerator, preferably overnight, and once it has thawed, use that day. Thawed fish can be a little wet, so wipe it with kitchen paper before cooking to remove some of the excess moisture. Never re-freeze thawed fish.

Preparing fish and shellfish

The preparation of fish, especially gutting and scaling, can be messy, so ask your fishmonger to do it for you, along with filleting fish.

Clams, mussels and cockles that are bad are easily spotted. If they are open before cooking and don't close when tapped or do not open when cooked, discard them. Likewise for any that have broken shells. Rinse mussels, clams and cockles under cold running water for a couple of minutes to remove some of the grit found in their shells.

Scallops are usually sold already cleaned by fishmongers: i.e. the white muscle and orange coral have already been removed from the shell. If you buy scallops still in their shells, you will need to remove the gills, which look like a feathery 'skirt' around the edge. To do this, remove the whole scallop (muscle, coral and skirt) from the shell by loosening the muscle with a sharp knife, then pull the skirt away from the muscle using your fingers.

Squid has a bad reputation, as it is often tough and rubbery, but that is because it has been cooked incorrectly. There is no middle ground when it comes to cooking squid: it should be very fast or very slow, and either method will result in beautifully tender squid. If cooking it quickly, you need to use a very, very hot pan and fry it for only a minute; alternatively, braise it slowly as though making a stew. Preparing squid is simpler than it looks, since it is bought part-prepared. Pull the tentacles out of the main body, where they will have been placed, and, if you want to use them, cut them from the head just below the eye. Now take the main sac or body, also known as a tube, and feel inside for a hard,

Mussels will generally need to be debearded at home. Simply pull the fibrous beards from the mussels. If they are a little stubborn, simply cut them off with a pair of scissors. Barnacles will also need to be scubbed off.

plastic-like quill. If one is there, pull it out and discard it. Now rinse the body out well, then either cut it down one side to open it out or just slice it into rings. If you are scoring the flesh to help tenderize it, always score the inside of the flesh.

Cooking fish

In most of the recipes in this book the fish takes only minutes to cook, and therefore it is important to get everything ready before it hits the pan. The most common mistake when cooking fish is to overcook it.

When pan-frying fillets of fish with the skin on, three-quarters of the cooking should be done on the skin side, as this protects the flesh and allows it to cook without becoming dry. You should be able to see that the fish is almost cooked, as it becomes opaque around the edges, before turning it over to cook the other side for a minute or so.

If you are unsure as to whether fish is cooked or not, insert the sharp point of a knife or a cocktail stick into the flesh. If it glides into the flesh easily, without resistance, then the fish is cooked. This is a handy tip when cooking thicker fillets or roasting fish. Cooked fish will also feel firm to the touch and be opaque in colour.

Essential flavours

Even if you have no time to go shopping, a few store-cupboard ingredients open up a whole world of flavours for quick and easy recipes from around the world. Dried ingredients such pasta, pulses and grains and

sauces such Thai fish sauce, soy sauce, sweet chilli sauce and harissa paste will all keep for months in the cupboard and refrigerator, and will help to make wonderful dishes.

There is a huge variety of spices on the market now, and adding a few of the essentials can result in wonderful curries and spiced stews in minutes. Make sure you always have coriander seeds, cumin seeds, fennel seeds, mustard seeds, turmeric, garam masala, paprika, smoked paprika and cayenne pepper in the cupboard. Red and green chillies freeze well for when you want to add a little more heat. Cans of tomatoes

and coconut milk are also essential for a quick curry or sauce. Cans and jars of olives, roasted peppers, sun-dried tomatoes, pulses and anchovies are other store-cupboard essentials.

Flavoured butters are a quick way to introduce flavours to fish that has been simply cooked. Make larger quantities than given in the recipes in this book and keep them in the freezer. Then simply cut a few slices from the roll of flavoured butter and allow it to melt on the fish.

Nutritional value of fish

Many nutritionists recommend that you eat fish at least twice a week due to its nutritional benefits. Fish is naturally low in saturated fat and high in the essential fats, especially in the case of oily fish such as salmon and mackerel. These oily fish are high in omega-3, a fatty acid that must be ingested, as the body cannot naturally produce it. Omega-3 is an important part of the diet for both children and adults because it is necessary for a healthy nervous system.

Fish is also naturally high in protein, which is needed in every cell of the body to build healthy bones, muscles, tendons and ligaments. There are also many vitamins, minerals and trace elements found in fish, which contribute to a healthy and balanced diet. Shellfish can be high in cholesterol, but this type of cholesterol doesn't make a great contribution to your blood cholesterol levels, and so shellfish need not be avoided on health grounds.

making fish stock

Why bother making your own stock? In an age when we are all being advised to cut down on our salt consumption, homemade stock can be salt-free; it also fits in with our aspiration to recycle all we can.

Fish can be expensive, so if you have bought a whole fish that the fishmonger is going to fillet for you, ask to keep the bones and heads to make your own stock. (Note that plaice bones make a bitter stock and so are not worth keeping.)

If you haven't got time to make stock now, don't throw the fish bones out – just pack them into a plastic bag and freeze them until you do have time. The following recipe makes 1 litres (1¾ pints).

If using frozen fish bones, make sure they are completely thawed before use. Don't try to speed up thawing by plunging them into warm water. Immerse in cold water and change the water frequently, or thaw in the microwave, following the manufacturer's guidelines. Stock can be frozen in ice cube trays then tipped into a bag and stored in the freezer for easy and convenient use.

Basic fish stock

500 g (1 lb) leftover **fish bones**

1.5 litres (2½ pints) water, or enough to cover the fish bones and vegetables

a few **vegetables**, such as **onion**, **celery**, **leek** and **carrot**, roughly chopped

a few **peppercorns**

1 **bay leaf**

a few **thyme sprigs**

a few **parsley stalks**

salt and **pepper**

Cover the bones with the water and add the vegetables, peppercorns, bay leaf, thyme and parsley. Bring the water to the boil, then reduce the heat and simmer for 20 minutes, removing any scum that comes to the surface.

Strain the stock, discarding the vegetables and bones, then place it over a high heat to reduce to the desired consistency and flavour.

Finally, season with salt and pepper.

nibbles

cured salmon & cucumber spoons

Serves **4**

Preparation time **15 minutes**,
plus marinating

250 g (8 oz) **skinless salmon
fillet**, pin-boned and
finely diced

4 tablespoons **lemon juice**

¼ **cucumber**, deseeded and
finely diced

2 tablespoons drained **capers**,
finely chopped

1 tablespoon finely chopped
tarragon

1 tablespoon **mayonnaise**

salt and **pepper**

a few **dill sprigs**, to garnish
(optional)

Place the salmon in a non-metallic bowl. Pour over
the lemon juice and toss the salmon in it until all the
pieces are coated. Cover and leave in the refrigerator
to marinate for 3 hours.

Drain off the excess lemon juice and discard. Mix the
salmon with the cucumber, capers, chopped tarragon
and mayonnaise, season with salt and pepper and serve
on silver or clear spoons topped with dill sprigs, if liked.

For smoked salmon with pickled cucumber, using
a Y-shaped peeler, peel the outer flesh of a cucumber
into ribbons, leaving the seeds behind. In a small
saucepan, bring 2 tablespoons rice vinegar and
1 tablespoon caster sugar to the boil. Remove from
the heat and leave to cool, then add to the cucumber
ribbons along with 1 tablespoon chopped dill. Serve
with smoked salmon.

sushi

Serves **4–6**

Preparation time **30 minutes**, plus cooling

Cooking time **15 minutes**

225 g (7½ oz) **sushi rice**

450 ml (¾ pint) **water**

4 **spring onions**, very finely shredded

4 tablespoons **seasoned rice vinegar**

1 tablespoon **caster sugar**

25 g (1 oz) **pickled ginger**, shredded

1 tablespoon **toasted sesame seeds**

3–4 **nori** sheets

100 g (3½ oz) very fresh **wild salmon**, sliced into small strips

1 large **skinless sole fillet**, pin-boned and sliced into small strips

10 **cooked peeled prawns**

light soy sauce, to serve

Put the rice in a heavy-based saucepan with the measurement water. Bring slowly to the boil, then reduce the heat and simmer, half-covered, for 5–8 minutes, or until all the water has been absorbed. Cover completely and cook very gently for a further 5 minutes, or until the rice is very tender and sticky. Turn into a bowl and leave to cool.

Stir the spring onions, vinegar, sugar, ginger and sesame seeds into the rice.

Use scissors to cut the nori sheets into 6 cm (2½ inch) squares. Dampen your hands and mould the rice into little ovals. Arrange the rice ovals diagonally over the nori squares.

Bring the pointed ends on opposite sides of the nori over the rice and arrange a piece of fish or a prawn on top. Arrange on a serving platter and serve with a small bowl of soy sauce for dipping.

For chilli & coriander dipping sauce, to serve as an alternative accompaniment, place 4 tablespoons of light soy sauce in a bowl. Add 1 tablespoon sesame oil and a little wasabi paste and mix well. Add 1 finely chopped red chilli, 1 teaspoon sesame seeds and 1 tablespoon finely chopped coriander leaves and stir well.

crisp fried seafood

Serves **4–6**
Preparation time **20 minutes**
Cooking time **5 minutes**

500 g (1 lb) **mixed seafood**,
   such as whitebait, skinned
   white fish and squid, cleaned
   (see page 12)
1 **spring onion**, finely chopped
1 **mild red chilli**, deseeded
   and thinly sliced
1 **garlic clove**, finely chopped
2 tablespoons chopped
   parsley
100 g (3½ oz) **semolina flour**
½ teaspoon **paprika**
sunflower oil, for deep-frying
salt and **pepper**
lemon or **lime wedges**,
   to serve

Cut the white fish into small chunks. Slice the squid into rings and pat dry on kitchen paper with the tentacles and any other seafood you might be using.

Mix the spring onion with the chilli, garlic, parsley and some salt. Set aside.

Put the semolina flour and paprika on a plate and season lightly with salt and pepper. Add the seafood and coat well.

Pour the oil into a deep-fat fryer or large saucepan to a depth of at least 7 cm (3 inches) and heat to 180–190°C (350–375°F), or until a cube of bread browns in 30 seconds. Fry the fish in batches for 30–60 seconds until crisp and golden. Drain on kitchen paper and keep warm while you cook the remainder. Serve in little dishes, sprinkled with the spring onion and herb mixture and accompanied by the lemon or lime wedges.

For sweet chilli mayonnaise, to serve as an accompaniment, mix 4 tablespoons mayonnaise with 1 tablespoon sweet chilli sauce. Squeeze the juice of ½ lemon into the mayonnaise and mix well. Add a little chopped chilli if you like it hot.

thai-spiced prawn toasts

Serves **4**

Preparation time **25 minutes**, plus cooling

Cooking time **20 minutes**

1 tablespoon **vegetable oil**

1 **onion**, finely chopped

1 **red chilli**, deseeded and finely chopped

5 cm (2 inch) piece of **fresh root ginger**, peeled and finely chopped

1 **garlic clove**, crushed

200 g (7 oz) **raw peeled prawns**

150 g (5 oz) **minced pork**

1 **egg**, lightly beaten

1 tablespoon **Thai fish sauce**

2 tablespoons chopped **coriander**, plus extra sprigs to garnish

finely grated rind of 2 **limes**

5 slices of **white bread**

2 tablespoons **sesame seeds**

vegetable oil, for deep-frying

salt and **pepper**

2 **limes**, cut into wedges, to garnish

Heat the oil in a frying pan over a medium heat, add the onion, chilli and ginger and fry until the onion is soft. Add the garlic and fry for a further minute. Set aside to cool.

Place the cooled onion mixture, prawns and pork in a food processor and blend until a paste is formed. Add the egg, fish sauce, coriander, lime rind and a little salt and pepper and blend once more.

Spread this mixture over the bread in a layer about 1 cm (½ inch) thick. Sprinkle with the sesame seeds and cut into neat triangles.

Pour the oil into a deep-fat fryer or large saucepan to a depth of at least 7 cm (3 inches) and heat to 180–190°C (350-375°F), or until a cube of bread browns in 30 seconds. Fry the prawn toasts in batches of 4 triangles at a time, prawn-side down first, for 3 minutes, then turn over and cook on the bread side for a further minute. The prawn toasts should be golden brown. Drain on kitchen paper and keep warm while you cook the remainder. Serve with lime slices to squeeze over the toasts, garnished with coriander sprigs.

For lime & chilli dipping sauce, to serve as an accompaniment, mix together 2 tablespoons lime juice, 2 tablespoons sweet chilli sauce and 2 tablespoons Thai fish sauce.

octopus with garlic dressing

Serves **6–8**

Preparation time **10 minutes**,
   plus cooling and chilling

Cooking time 1½ **hours**

1 **onion**, cut into wedges

1 teaspoon **whole cloves**

2 litres (3½ pints) **water**

500 g (1 lb) **prepared
   octopus**, bought at least
   2 days before being cooked,
   and placed in the freezer
   for 48 hours to tenderize
   the meat

6 tablespoons **extra virgin
   olive oil**

2 **garlic cloves**, crushed

4 tablespoons chopped
   parsley

1 teaspoon **white wine
   vinegar**

salt and **pepper**

Put the onion, cloves and 1 tablespoon salt in a large saucepan and add the measurement water. Bring to the boil. Using tongs, dip the octopus in and out of the water about 4 times, returning the water to the boil before re-dipping, then immerse the octopus completely in the water. (This helps to make the flesh tender.) If there are several pieces of octopus, dip them 1 at a time.

Reduce the heat and cook the octopus very gently for 1 hour, then check to see whether it's tender. Cook for a further 15–30 minutes if necessary. Leave it to cool in the liquid, then drain, cut into bite-sized pieces and place a non-metallic bowl.

Mix the oil with the garlic, parsley, vinegar and salt and pepper to taste and add to the bowl. Mix well, cover and chill for several hours or overnight. Serve the octopus with bread for mopping up the juices.

For octopus with spicy chorizo, cook the octopus as above, then leave to cool; cut into bite-sized pieces. Sprinkle 2 sliced chorizo sausages with 1 teaspoon sweet paprika and fry until crispy. Drain on kitchen paper to remove the excess oil. Place 2 tablespoons olive oil in a bowl with the juice of 1 lemon and the chorizo. Season with salt and pepper. Add the octopus and mix well to coat in the oil. When you are ready to serve, stir in 1 tablespoon chopped coriander leaves and 1 tablespoon chopped parsley. Serve with bread.

salt cod pâté with crostini

Serves **4**

Preparation time **15 minutes**, plus soaking, cooling and chilling

Cooking time **15 minutes**

300 g (10 oz) pieces of **salt cod**

1 **garlic clove**, crushed

100 ml (3½ fl oz) **double cream**

½ teaspoon **paprika**

lemon juice, to taste

pepper

small bunch of **chives**, finely chopped, to garnish (optional)

Crostini

5 slices of **Granary bread**

olive oil

Cover the salt cod in cold water and leave to soak for 12 hours, changing the water as often as possible.

Place the soaked salt cod in a saucepan and cover with fresh cold water. Bring to the boil, then reduce the heat and simmer for 5 minutes. Drain. When cool enough to handle, flake the fish into a food processor, removing the bones and skin. Add the garlic and blend. While the motor is running, pour in the cream. Remove from the processor and season with paprika, lemon juice and pepper. Salt will most likely not be needed. Place the pâté in a bowl and cover with clingfilm. Once cool, place in the refrigerator for at least 1 hour.

Make the crostini by stamping out 4 x 3 cm (1¼ inch) rounds from each slice of bread using a biscuit or pastry cutter. Place them on a baking sheet, drizzle with a little olive oil and cook for 7–10 minutes in a preheated oven, 180°C (350°F), Gas Mark 4, until golden and crispy.

Spread the salt cod pâté on the crostini and sprinkle with finely chopped chives, if liked.

For salt cod with pepper salsa, soak and boil 300 g (10 oz) salt cod as above. Once cooked, flake the fish into small pieces and fry in a little olive oil until crispy. Chop 200 g (7 oz) mixed marinated peppers (from a jar) and mix with a little of their own oil. Add 8 drained and chopped sun-dried tomatoes in oil and 8 chopped pitted black olives. Serve the pepper mixture on little crostini, made as above, and top with a few flakes of salt cod and a squeeze of lemon.

salt & chilli squid

Serves **6–8**

Preparation time **20 minutes**, plus chilling

Cooking time **3 minutes**

750 g (1½ lb) **squid**, cleaned (see page 12) and halved lengthways, tentacles discarded

200 ml (7 fl oz) **lemon juice**

100 g (3½ oz) **cornflour**

1½ tablespoons **salt**

2 teaspoons **white pepper**

1 teaspoon **chilli powder**

2 teaspoons **caster sugar**

4 **egg whites**, lightly beaten

sunflower oil, for deep-frying

Dipping sauce

1 **red chilli**, deseeded and finely diced

1 tablespoon diced **shallot**

2 teaspoons very finely chopped **coriander**

6 tablespoons **light soy sauce**

1 tablespoon **Chinese rice wine**

To garnish

red chillies, deseeded and finely sliced

spring onions, finely sliced

Open the squid out and pat dry with kitchen paper. Lay them on a chopping board, shiny-side down, and, using a sharp knife, lightly score a fine diamond pattern on the flesh, being careful not to cut all the way through. Cut the squid into 5 x 2 cm (2 x 1 inch) pieces and place in a non-metallic dish. Pour over the lemon juice, cover and chill for 15 minutes.

Combine the cornflour, salt, pepper, chilli powder and sugar in a bowl. Dip the squid pieces into the beaten egg whites and then into the cornflour mixture, shaking off any excess.

Pour the oil into a deep-fat fryer or large saucepan to a depth of at least 7 cm (3 inches) and heat to 180–190°C (350–375°F), or until a cube of bread browns in 30 seconds. Deep-fry the squid in 3 batches for 1 minute, or until it turns pale golden and curls up. Remove each batch with a slotted spoon and drain on kitchen paper.

Mix all the ingredients for the dipping sauce in a bowl. Serve the squid in small paper cones, if liked, garnished with sliced red chilli and spring onions and accompanied by the dipping sauce.

For salt & pepper squid, prepare the squid as above. Mix together 100 g (3½ oz) cornflour, 2 teaspoons caster sugar, 1½ tablespoons salt, 1 teaspoon ground white pepper and 1 teaspoon ground black pepper. Dip the squid into lightly beaten egg white and then into the cornflour mixture. Deep-fry in sunflower oil for 1 minute, then drain on kitchen paper and serve as above.

spicy tuna skewers

Serves **4**

Preparation time **10 minutes**, plus marinating

Cooking time **6 minutes**

1 tablespoon **turmeric**

1 tablespoon **ground cumin**

1 tablespoon **ground coriander**

3.5 cm (1½ inch) piece of **fresh root ginger**, peeled and finely chopped

2 tablespoons **olive oil**

2 **garlic cloves**, crushed

400 g (13 oz) **fresh tuna steak**, cut in to chunks

200 ml (7 fl oz) **natural yogurt**

finely grated rind of 1 **lemon**

vegetable oil, for brushing

salt and **pepper**

Put the turmeric, cumin, coriander, ginger, olive oil and 1 of the garlic cloves in a bowl and stir well. Add the tuna, coating all the pieces with the mix. Cover and leave in the refrigerator to marinate for at least 1 hour, preferably overnight.

Mix the yogurt with the remaining garlic clove and the lemon rind and season with salt and pepper. Heat a griddle pan over a high heat and brush with a little vegetable oil. Sear the tuna pieces in batches for 1 minute on 1 side and 30 seconds on the other. Remove from the pan and serve with bamboo skewers for dipping into the yogurt sauce.

For seared tuna with wasabi mayonnaise, rub 400 g (13 oz) fresh tuna steak, cut into chunks, with a little vegetable oil. Season with salt and a little ground Sichuan pepper, then sear in a hot griddle pan as above. Mix together 5 tablespoons mayonnaise with 1 tablespoon wasabi paste and 1 teaspoon lime juice. Serve with the seared tuna.

herring & dilled-cucumber skewers

Makes **15**

Preparation time **15 minutes**, plus chilling

15 canned or bottled **pickled herring fillets (matjes)**, drained, or 15 **roll-mop herrings**

Dilled cucumber

1 large **cucumber**

200 ml (7 fl oz) **white wine vinegar**

2 teaspoons **caster sugar**

3 tablespoons finely chopped **dill**

salt and **pepper**

Pink beetroot & soured cream dipping sauce, to serve (optional – see below)

Cut the cucumber into long, thin slices using a vegetable peeler and put them in a shallow, non-metallic bowl. Mix the vinegar with the sugar, stir in the dill and pour over the cucumber. Season well with salt and pepper, cover and leave to pickle in the refrigerator for 3–4 hours.

Thread a herring fillet or roll-mop herring on to a wooden or bamboo skewer with some of the cucumber slices. Repeat with the remaining herring and cucumber to give you 15 skewers. Serve at room temperature with the Pink Beetroot & Soured Cream Dipping Sauce (see below), if liked.

For pink beetroot & soured cream dipping sauce, to serve as an accompaniment, finely grate 50 g (2 oz) cooked, peeled beetroot in a food processor. Add 100 ml (3½ fl oz) soured cream and 100 g (3½ oz) mayonnaise and blend until fairly smooth and pink, then chill until ready to use.

cajun calamari with avocado dip

Serves **4**
Preparation time **7 minutes**
Cooking time **8 minutes**

150 g (5 oz) **plain flour**
1 heaped tablespoon **Cajun seasoning**
4 large **squid**, cleaned (see page 12) and cut into rings, tentacles discarded
vegetable oil, for shallow-frying
salt and **pepper**

Avocado dip
2 ripe **avocados**, peeled and stoned
1 small **red onion**, finely chopped
1 **red chilli**, deseeded and finely chopped
2 tablespoons **double cream**
juice of 1 **lime**

Put the avocados in a food processor and blend until smooth (or simply mash with a fork). Stir in the onion, chilli and cream and season with the lime juice, salt and pepper. Set aside while you prepare and cook the calamari.

Put the flour and Cajun seasoning in a large freezer bag along with a little salt and pepper. Mix well. Add the squid to the bag and shake well to coat all the squid in the flour mixture.

Heat 1 cm (½ inch) oil in a frying pan over a high heat. Shake off the excess flour and fry the squid quickly in small batches for 1–2 minutes. Remove from the pan and drain on kitchen paper. Keep warm while you cook the remainder, then serve immediately with the avocado dip.

For breaded lime prawns with chilli mayonnaise,
take 20 large raw prawns, peeled but tails left on. Dust with plain flour, then dip in beaten egg and finally roll in panko breadcrumbs (Japanese breadcrumbs) or dried white breadcrumbs if panko are unavailable. Shallow-fry in vegetable oil until golden, then squeeze over the juice of 1 lime. Mix 1 deseeded and finely chopped red chilli with 125 g (4 oz) mayonnaise and serve with the lime prawns.

crispy whitebait & chip cones

Makes **12** cones
Preparation time **20 minutes**
Cooking time **10 minutes**

250 g (8 oz) **potatoes**, peeled
    and cut into long, thin chips
sunflower oil, for deep-frying
4 tablespoons **plain flour**
400 g (13 oz) **whitebait**
salt and **pepper**
malt vinegar, to serve

Line a large sheet of newspaper with greaseproof
paper, cut the double layer into 12 squares and twist
each into a small cone.

Rinse the chips in cold water and dry thoroughly on
kitchen paper. Pour the oil into a deep-fat fryer or large
saucepan to a depth of at least 7 cm (3 inches) and
heat to 180–190°C (350–375°F), or until a cube of
bread browns in 30 seconds. Deep-fry the chips for
4–5 minutes, then drain on kitchen paper and deep-fry
them again for 1–2 minutes until crisp and golden.
Drain the chips and keep them warm.

Put the flour on a large plate and season well with salt
and pepper. Toss the whitebait in the flour and fry in
batches for 1–2 minutes, or until crisp and golden.
Drain on kitchen paper.

Toss the whitebait with the chips, season with salt
and pile into the paper cones. Serve the malt vinegar
on the side.

For whitebait with Indian spiced sweet potato
wedges, peel 2 large sweet potatoes and cut into
wedges. Place in a bowl with 2 tablespoons vegetable
oil, 1 teaspoon ground cumin, 1 teaspoon ground
coriander and 1 teaspoon lightly crushed fennel seeds
and toss together. Spread on a nonstick baking tray
and roast in a preheated oven, 200° C (400° F), Gas
Mark 6, for 30 minutes until tender in the centre and
crispy on the outside. Meanwhile, cook the whitebait
as above, then serve tossed with the potato wedges.

sweetcorn fritters with john dory

Serves **4**
Preparation time **10 minutes**
Cooking time **20 minutes**

2 tablespoons **olive oil**
2 **John Dory**, filleted, pin-
    boned and cut into bite-sized
    pieces
salt and **pepper**

Fritters
75 g (3 oz) **self-raising flour**
½ teaspoon **paprika**
1 **egg**
50 ml (2 fl oz) **milk**
2 **sweetcorn cobs**, kernels
    removed
1 **red pepper**, cored,
    deseeded and finely diced
2 tablespoons **vegetable oil**

To serve (optional)
100 g (3½ oz) **soured cream**
a few **coriander leaves**

Mix together the flour, paprika, egg and milk to make a thick, smooth batter. Fold in the sweetcorn and red pepper and season with salt and pepper.

Heat the vegetable oil in a frying pan over a medium heat. Drop in heaped teaspoonfuls of the fritter mixture and fry until golden and bubbles start to appear on the surface. Turn over and cook on the other side until brown. Keep warm while cooking the fish. (Alternatively, the fritters can also be made the day before and heated in the oven before serving.)

Heat a frying pan over a high heat and add the olive oil. Season the fish and fry for 2 minutes until the skin is golden and crispy, then turn over and cook for a further 30 seconds. Place a piece of fish on each fritter, topped with a spoonful of soured cream and garnished with a coriander leaf, if liked.

For sweetcorn & pepper spoons with John Dory, mix together 250 g (8 oz) canned, drained sweetcorn and 1 cored, deseeded and finely chopped red pepper. Add 1 teaspoon finely chopped red chilli, 1 tablespoon chopped coriander and 1 tablespoon olive oil. Season with salt and pepper. Fry the John Dory as above. Place a little of the sweetcorn mixture into a silver dessert spoon and top with a piece of the fish and a squeeze of lime. Garnish with a coriander sprig.

prosciutto & scallop kebabs

Makes **20**
Preparation time **20 minutes**,
 plus marinating
Cooking time **2–4 minutes**

2 **garlic cloves**, crushed
1 **dried red chilli**, crushed
4 tablespoons **olive oil**
juice of ½ **orange**
1 teaspoon **dried oregano**
20 cleaned **king scallops**,
 corals removed (optional)
10 thin slices of **prosciutto**,
 each cut into 2 strips
20 **basil leaves**
20 **sun-blushed tomato**
 halves
salt

Put the garlic, chilli, oil, orange juice and oregano in a small bowl, mix well and season with salt.

Arrange the scallops in a single layer in a shallow bowl and pour over the garlic and chilli mixture. Cover and leave in the refrigerator to marinate for 15–20 minutes.

Wrap a strip of prosciutto around each scallop and secure with a metal skewer or presoaked bamboo skewer. Add a basil leaf and a sun-blushed tomato half to each skewer.

Position the skewers about 6 cm (2½ inches) away from a grill preheated to high and cook for 1–2 minutes on each side, or until the scallops have just cooked through. (Do not overcook or the scallops will become tough.) Remove from the grill and serve immediately.

For citrus dressing, to serve as an accompaniment, place the juice of ½ orange and ½ grapefruit in a small saucepan. Bring to the boil and reduce until thick and syrupy. Pour into a bowl and whisk in 3 tablespoons olive oil. Season with salt and pepper and add a little honey if the dressing is too sharp.

smoked salmon & cucumber sushi

Serves **4**

Preparation time **15 minutes**,
  plus cooling

Cooking time **15 minutes**

300 g (10 oz) **sushi rice**

2 tablespoons **rice vinegar**

1 tablespoon **caster sugar**

2 **nori sheets**

1 teaspoon **wasabi paste**

2 long strips of **cucumber**, the
  length of the nori and about
  1 cm (½ inch) thick

100 g (3½ oz) **smoked
  salmon**

2 tablespoons **pickled ginger**

4 tablespoons **soy sauce**

Cook the sushi rice according to the instructions on
the packet.

Mix together the vinegar and sugar and stir until the
sugar dissolves. Once the rice is cooked and when
it is still warm, mix in enough of the vinegar and sugar
mixture to coat the rice grains, but do not allow the rice
to become wet. Tip the rice on to a tray to cool quickly.

Take 1 nori sheet and place it on a bamboo mat with
the longest side in line with your body and the ridged
surface facing upwards. With damp hands, cover three-
quarters of the nori sheet with a thin layer of rice,
leaving a band of nori at the top without rice.

Spread a little wasabi paste with your finger on top of
the rice in a thin line, at the edge nearest to you. Then
place a cucumber strip and some smoked salmon on top.

Use the bamboo mat to start rolling the nori up, tucking
in the cucumber and salmon as you go. Once you have
rolled up the majority of the nori, wet your finger and
dampen the plain edge of nori. Finish rolling up the nori
and the wet edge will stick the roll together. Repeat
with the other nori sheet. Then, using a sharp knife, cut
the rolls into 8 even pieces.

Mix the remaining wasabi with the pickled ginger and
soy sauce and serve alongside the nori rolls.

chilli crab on mini noodle nests

Makes **20**
Preparation time **10 minutes**
Cooking time **11−15 minutes**

100 g (3½ oz) **fresh fine egg noodles**

1 tablespoon **sunflower oil**, plus extra for greasing

2 **spring onions**, finely sliced

2 **garlic cloves**, finely chopped

1 teaspoon peeled and finely diced **fresh root ginger**

1 **red chilli**, deseeded and finely diced

200 g (7 oz) **fresh white crabmeat**

2 tablespoons **sweet chilli sauce**

4 tablespoons finely chopped **coriander**

Grease 20 nonstick mini tartlet cases lightly with oil. Divide the noodles into 20 portions and press each portion into a tartlet case to form a tartlet shape, making sure the base is covered. Lightly brush with more oil and put in a preheated oven, 180°C (350°F), Gas Mark 4, for 8−10 minutes, or until crisp and firm. Remove from the cases and leave to cool on a wire rack.

Heat the 1 tablespoon oil in a large, nonstick wok or frying pan and add the spring onions, garlic, ginger and chilli and stir-fry for 2−3 minutes. Add the crabmeat and stir-fry for a further 1−2 minutes, then remove from the heat, stir in the sweet chilli sauce and coriander and toss to mix well.

Place a heaped teaspoonful of the chilli crab mixture into each cooled noodle nest and serve immediately.

For chilli crab linguine, cook 300 g (10 oz) linguine according to the instructions on the packet. Drain and set aside. Heat 2 tablespoons olive oil in a large frying pan and fry 1 finely chopped large red chilli for 2 minutes. Stir in 4 finely sliced spring onions, 375 g (12 oz) fresh white crabmeat, the juice of 1 lime and 2 tablespoons roughly chopped coriander leaves and warm through. Add the linguine and toss all the ingredients together. Dress the crab linguine with 2 tablespoons olive oil and serve immediately.

sweet chilli & ginger pollock

Serves **4**
Preparation time **15 minutes**
Cooking time **20 minutes**

150 g (5 oz) **self-raising flour**
1 tablespoon **cornflour**
2 tablespoons chopped
  coriander
125 ml (4 fl oz) **sparkling**
  water
425 g (14 oz) **pollock fillet**,
  pin-boned and cut into
  7 x 2.5 cm (3 x 1 inch) strips
vegetable oil, for deep-frying
salt and **pepper**
1 **lime**, cut into wedges,
  to garnish

Sauce
50 ml (2 fl oz) **sweet chilli**
  sauce
1 tablespoon finely chopped
  pickled ginger, plus
  1 teaspoon of the juice

Mix the sauce ingredients together and set aside.

Place the flour, cornflour, coriander and a good pinch of salt and pepper in a large bowl. Using a fork, stir in the sparkling water to make a batter of the consistency of double cream. Do not overstir the batter: small lumps of flour are fine. Pat the fish strips dry on kitchen paper and dip into the batter.

Pour the oil into a deep-fat fryer or large saucepan to a depth of at least 7 cm (3 inches) and heat to 180–190°C (350–375°F), or until a cube of bread browns in 30 seconds. Cook the fish in small batches until it is golden brown. Drain on kitchen paper and keep warm while you cook the remainder.

Serve the goujons with the sauce, garnished with the lime wedges.

For homemade tartare sauce, to serve as an alternative accompaniment, mix together 150 ml (¼ pint) mayonnaise, 1 tablespoon each gherkins, capers and shallot, all finely chopped, and 2 tablespoons chopped parsley. Season with salt and pepper.

anchovy puff pastry straws

Serves **4**

Preparation time **10 minutes**

Cooking time **10 minutes**

2 sheets of **ready-rolled puff pastry**, thawed if frozen

50 g (2 oz) **canned anchovy fillets**, drained and finely chopped

4 tablespoons finely grated **Parmesan cheese**

1 **egg**, lightly beaten

1 tablespoon **black sesame seeds**

Lay 1 sheet of the puff pastry on the work surface. Spread the anchovies over it and sprinkle with the Parmesan.

Brush the top of the other sheet of pastry with a little beaten egg. Place this on top of the anchovy and cheese mixture, egg wash-side down, to make a puff pastry sandwich. Roll over the puff pastry sandwich with a rolling pin to seal the 2 sheets together. It should be about the same thickness as 1 of the original sheets of pastry. Brush the top of the sandwich with a little beaten egg and sprinkle with a few black sesame seeds.

Cut the sandwich into 10 x 1.5 cm (4 x ¾ inch) strips and place on a nonstick baking sheet, leaving room between them to allow them to expand.

Place the straws in a preheated oven, 200°C (400°F), Gas Mark 6, and bake for 10 minutes, or until risen and golden brown. Remove from the oven and cool on a wire rack.

For anchovy & black olive filo pastry straws, take 1 sheet of filo pastry and brush it with a little melted butter. Place another sheet on top and brush with melted butter. Mix together 50 g (2 oz) canned, drained anchovy fillets and 50 g (2 oz) chopped pitted black olives. Spread a little of this mixture at the edge of the filo pastry, then start to roll it up into a straw shape. Cut each straw in half. Brush the outside of the straws with more melted butter and bake in a preheated oven, 190°C (375°F), Gas Mark 5, for 8–10 minutes, or until golden brown.

lobster & tarragon puffs

Makes **20**
Preparation time **20 minutes**
Cooking time **12–15 minutes**

200 g (7 oz) **puff pastry**,
  thawed if frozen
plain flour, for dusting
2 **eggs**, lightly beaten for
  glazing
150 g (5 oz) **cooked lobster
  tail meat**, chopped into 1 cm
  (½ inch) dice
4 tablespoons **mayonnaise**
1 teaspoon **American-style
  mustard**
1 tablespoon cored, deseeded
  and very finely diced **red
  pepper**
2 tablespoons very finely
  chopped **tarragon**
salt and **pepper**
tarragon sprigs, to garnish

Line a large baking sheet with nonstick baking paper. Roll the pastry out on a lightly floured surface to 5 mm (¼ inch) thick. Stamp out 40 x 6 cm (2½ inch) rounds using a biscuit or pastry cutter. Put 20 of the rounds on the baking sheet, spaced well apart, and brush with beaten egg. Using a 3 cm (1¼ inch) cutter, stamp out circles from the centre of the remaining rounds. Discard the inner pastry circles, leaving you with 20 pastry 'rings'. Put these 'rings' on the brushed pastry rounds and press gently to seal. Brush again with the beaten egg, then bake in a preheated oven, 200°C (400°F), Gas Mark 6, for 12–15 minutes, or until risen and golden. Remove from the oven and transfer to a wire rack to cool completely.

Meanwhile, put the lobster meat in a bowl and mix in the mayonnaise, mustard, red pepper and chopped tarragon. Season well with salt and pepper. Using a teaspoon, carefully spoon the mixture into the cold puff shells. Garnish with tarragon sprigs and serve immediately.

For prawns wrapped in puff pastry blankets, roll out 200 g (7 oz) puff pastry until it is 2–3 mm (⅛ inch) thick. Take 15 large raw king prawns and remove their heads and shells, leaving the very end of the tails on. Cut the sheet of puff pastry into 5 cm (2 inch) squares. Brush the edges with a little beaten egg. Wrap each prawn in a pastry square, leaving the end of the tail exposed. Trim any excess pastry. Brush the tops with beaten egg and sprinkle with sesame seeds. Bake in a preheated oven, 180° C (350° F), Gas Mark 4, for 10–15 minutes until golden brown.

crayfish rolls with hoisin sauce

Serves **4**

Preparation time **25 minutes**

8 **rice paper sheets**

16 long **chives**

4 **iceberg lettuce leaves**,
  finely shredded

4 **spring onions**, finely
  shredded into matchsticks

16 **mint leaves**, shredded

16 **cooked peeled crayfish
  tails**

3 tablespoons **hoisin sauce**

Fill a shallow bowl with hot water and soak the rice
paper sheets for around 5 minutes until softened.
Remove the sheets from the water and place on a
clean, dry tea towel. Cut in half.

Blanch the chives in boiling water for 10 seconds, then
cool under cold running water.

Take 1 half sheet of rice paper and fill with a little
lettuce, spring onions, mint and a crayfish tail. Roll the
rice paper sheet to enclose these ingredients, folding in
the ends to enclose everything. Tie a chive around the
centre of the roll to seal it closed, then place on a tray
covered with a clean, damp tea towel while you make
the remaining rolls. Serve the crayfish rolls with the
hoisin sauce for dipping.

For prawn & bamboo shoot spring rolls, brush
1 sheet of filo pastry with a little melted butter. With
the short side of the pastry in line with your body,
place 1 raw peeled king prawn and a small pile of
bamboo shoots in the centre of the pastry at the edge.
Roll the filo pastry sheet to enclose these ingredients,
folding in the ends to enclose everything. Repeat with
15 more sheets of filo pastry, 15 more prawns and
some bamboo shoots. Brush the spring rolls with
melted butter and bake in a preheated oven, 180°C
(350°F), Gas Mark 4, for 10–15 minutes until golden
brown. Serve with hoisin sauce for dipping.

soba, tobiko & spring onion spoons

Makes **20**
Preparation time **15 minutes**
Cooking time **5 minutes**

250 g (8 oz) **dried soba noodles**
4 tablespoons **light soy sauce**
4 tablespoons **mirin** (rice wine)
1 teaspoon **toasted sesame oil**
¼ teaspoon **wasabi paste**
6 tablespoons **sunflower oil**
2 **spring onions**, very finely sliced
25 g (1 oz) **tobiko** (flying fish roe) or small salmon roe

Cook the noodles according to the instructions on the packet until just tender. Drain, rinse in cold water and drain again.

Whisk the soy sauce with the mirin, sesame oil, wasabi paste and sunflower oil in a bowl until well blended. Add the noodles and toss gently to coat evenly, then stir in the spring onions and toss to mix well.

Divide the noodles into 20 bite-sized portions and twirl each portion with a fork to make a neat nest. Carefully transfer to individual oriental soup spoons, then, using a teaspoon, top each nest with a little tobiko or salmon roe and serve immediately.

For soba noodle & crayfish salad, cook the noodles according to the instructions on the packet, drain and set aside. Mix together 2 tablespoons sweet chilli sauce, the juice of 1 lime and 2 tablespoons Thai fish sauce. Pour the sauce over the drained noodles and mix well. Add 50 g (2 oz) salted peanuts, 200 g (7 oz) cooked peeled crayfish tails and 4 sliced spring onions, and serve garnished with a large handful of coriander leaves.

rosemary scones & smoked trout

Serves **4**

Preparation time **30 minutes**

Cooking time **7–10 minutes**

250 g (8 oz) **self-raising flour**, plus extra for dusting

pinch of **salt**

½ teaspoon **baking powder**

50 g (2 oz) **butter**, diced

1 tablespoon finely chopped **rosemary**

1 **egg**, lightly beaten

around 150 ml (¼ pint) **buttermilk**

milk, for glazing

a few **dill sprigs**, to garnish (optional)

Topping

125 g (4 oz) **cream cheese**

1 tablespoon chopped **dill**

1 tablespoon chopped **chives**

150 g (5 oz) **smoked trout**

salt and **pepper**

Sift the flour, salt and baking powder into a bowl and rub in the butter with your fingertips until the mixture resembles breadcrumbs. Stir in the rosemary, egg and enough buttermilk to give a soft but not sticky dough. Don't overwork the mixture.

Roll the dough out on a lightly floured surface to a thickness of 1.5 cm (¾ inch). Using a 3 cm (1¼ inch) biscuit or pastry cutter, cut out 16 rounds. Place them on a nonstick baking sheet and brush the tops with a little milk. Place them in a preheated oven, 190°C (375°F), Gas Mark 5, for 7–10 minutes, or until golden brown and risen, then transfer to a wire rack to cool.

Mix together the cream cheese, dill and chives and season with salt and pepper.

Cut the top off each scone to give a flat surface, then spread a little of the cream cheese mixture on top. Place a little smoked trout on the cream cheese mixture and garnish with a dill sprig, if liked.

For smoked salmon pâté, to serve as an alternative topping for the scones, blend 250 g (8 oz) smoked salmon with 2 tablespoons cream and 100 g (3½ oz) cream cheese in a food processor. Stir in 2 tablespoons chopped dill and season with salt and pepper.

potted shrimp with herby pittas

Serves **4**

Preparation time **10 minutes**, plus chilling

Cooking time **15 minutes**

1 tablespoon **olive oil**

1 small **red onion**, finely chopped

1 **green chilli**, deseeded and finely chopped

200 g (7 oz) **butter**

200 g (7 oz) **cooked peeled brown shrimps**

grated rind of **1 lime**, and about 1 teaspoon juice

salt and **pepper**

Herby pittas

50 g (2 oz) **butter**, softened

1 **garlic clove**, crushed

1 tablespoon finely chopped **coriander**

1 tablespoon finely chopped **parsley**

4 white or wholemeal **pitta breads**

Heat the oil in a frying pan over a medium heat. Add the onion and chilli and fry until the onion is soft and translucent. Remove from the heat, add the butter and let it melt. Finally, add the shrimps and lime rind. Season the shrimps with a squeeze of lime juice to taste and some salt and pepper.

Spoon the mixture into individual ramekins or a large serving ramekin. Cover and place in the refrigerator for at least 2 hours, or until the butter has set. (This can easily be done the day before.) Remove from the refrigerator 20 minutes before serving.

Place the softened butter in a small bowl. Mix in the garlic, coriander and parsley and season to taste with salt and pepper. Make a cut in each pitta bread to open up the pocket inside and spread with 1 teaspoon of the butter mixture.

Wrap the pitta breads in foil and place in a preheated oven, 180°C (350°F), Gas Mark 4, for 8–10 minutes, or until warmed through and the butter has melted. Serve with the potted shrimps.

For traditional potted shrimps, melt 200 g (7 oz) butter in a saucepan. Remove from the heat and stir in a pinch each of ground mace, nutmeg and paprika. Add 200 g (7 oz) cooked peeled brown shrimps, season with salt and pepper and pour into individual ramekins, then chill. Serve with toasted sourdough.

soups & stews

onion & bean soup with prawns

Serves **4**

Preparation time **25 minutes**

Cooking time **20 minutes**

2 tablespoons **olive oil**

10 **spring onions**, roughly
chopped, plus extra, finely
chopped to garnish

1 **garlic clove**, roughly
chopped

a few **thyme leaves**

2 x 400 g (13 oz) cans **butter
beans**, drained and rinsed

750 ml (1¼ pints) **chicken
stock** or **Basic Fish Stock**
(see page 15)

100 ml (3½ fl oz) **double
cream**

20 **raw peeled tiger prawns**,
deveined

salt and **pepper**

2 tablespoons finely chopped
chives, to garnish

Heat 1 tablespoon of the oil in a saucepan. Add the
roughly chopped spring onions, garlic and thyme leaves
and fry over a gentle heat until soft. Add the beans,
stock and cream. Bring the soup to the boil, then
reduce the heat and simmer for 5 minutes.

Transfer the soup to a liquidizer or food processor and
blend until smooth. If it is a little thick, add a little more
cream or stock. Season the soup with salt and pepper.

Place a frying pan over a high heat and add the
remaining oil. Season the prawns with salt and
pepper, then fry them in the pan for 4 minutes, or
until they turn pink.

Stack the prawns in the centre of 4 bowls and pour the
soup around them. Garnish the dish with a few chopped
spring onions and the chives.

For scallops with white bean purée, heat a little
olive oil in a pan. Gently fry 1 finely chopped onion
and 1 crushed garlic clove. Add 2 x 400 g (13 oz)
cans butter beans, drained and rinsed, and 50 ml
(2 oz) double cream to the pan to warm through.
Transfer the mixture to a liquidizer or food processor
and blend to form a rough or smooth purée, depending
on taste. A little more cream may be needed. Season
to taste. Heat 1 tablespoon olive oil in a frying pan
over a very high heat. Season 12 cleaned scallops
with a little salt, pepper and mild curry powder, then
fry for 1 minute on each side. Serve on top of the bean
purée with a rocket salad dressed with a little lemon
juice and olive oil.

spiced monkfish & chickpea stew

Serves **4**
Preparation time **10 minutes**
Cooking time **20 minutes**

2 tablespoons **vegetable oil**
1 **onion**, finely chopped
2 **garlic cloves**, crushed
¼ teaspoon **chilli powder**
1 tablespoon **curry powder**
¼ teaspoon **turmeric**
1 tablespoon **tomato purée**
2 x 400 g (13 oz) cans
   tomatoes
100 ml (3½ fl oz) **chicken
   stock** or **Basic Fish Stock**
   (see page 15)
750 g (1½ lb) **monkfish tail**,
   cut into large chunks
400 g (13 oz) can **chickpeas**,
   drained
1 tablespoon **Homemade
   Mango Chutney** (see page
   122)
4 tablespoons **natural yogurt**
large handful of **coriander
   leaves**
salt and **pepper**

Heat the oil in a large saucepan. Add the onion and fry gently until soft but not coloured. Add the garlic, chilli powder, curry powder and turmeric to the pan and fry for 2 minutes until the spices become fragrant. Add the tomato purée, tomatoes and stock and bring to the boil, then reduce the heat and simmer for 10 minutes. If the stew becomes too dry, add a little more stock.

Stir in the monkfish and chickpeas and bring to the boil, then reduce the heat and simmer for 5 minutes, or until the monkfish is cooked. Finally, stir in the mango chutney and season to taste with a little salt and pepper. Serve in bowls, topped with a spoonful of yogurt and some coriander leaves.

For cumin- & fennel-spiced chapatis, to serve as an accompaniment, sift together 100 g (3½ oz) plain flour and 100 g (3½ oz) wholemeal flour, discarding any bits of bran left in the sieve. Gently toast 1 tablespoon each cumin seeds and fennel seeds in a pan, then crush them using a pestle and mortar. Add the crushed spices to the flour with a good pinch of salt. Mix in enough water to give you a smooth dough. Wrap the dough in clingfilm and leave to rest for 1 hour. Heat a frying pan over a high heat. Divide the dough into 8 pieces and form into balls. Roll 1 of the balls into a thin, flat disc. Place in the pan for 40 seconds, flipping it a few times. Repeat with the rest of the dough. Keep the chapatis warm in a clean tea towel.

crab bisque with garlic croutons

Serves **4**

Preparation time **12 minutes**

Cooking time **40 minutes**

shells of 2 large **crabs**

4 tablespoons **olive oil**

1 **onion**, chopped

2 **carrots**, chopped

2 **celery sticks**, chopped

1 **bay leaf**

2 tablespoons **Cognac**

4 ripe **tomatoes**, roughly
chopped

2 teaspoons **tomato purée**

1 litre (1¾ pints) **Basic Fish
Stock** (see page 15)

2 **garlic cloves**, finely chopped

4 thick slices of **white bread**,
crusts removed and cut into
1 cm (½ inch) cubes

100 ml (3½ fl oz) **double
cream**

pinch of **cayenne pepper**

salt and **pepper**

Break up the crab shells using the back of a large knife and a mallet.

Heat 2 tablespoons of the oil in a large saucepan. Add the onion, carrots, celery and bay leaf and fry until soft but not coloured. Add the broken shells and fry for 2–3 minutes, then add the Cognac, tomatoes and tomato purée.

Pour in the stock and bring to the boil, then reduce the heat and simmer for 30 minutes.

Heat the remaining oil in a frying pan and add the garlic. Fry for 1 minute to flavour the oil, then remove and discard the garlic. Add the bread cubes to the garlic oil and fry until golden brown.

Remove the claw shell from the pan. Place the rest of the shells and liquid in a liquidizer or food processor in batches and blend until the shells are in pieces of about 1 cm (½ inch). Pass the liquid and shells through a fine sieve lined with a piece of muslin.

Pour the liquid back into a clean saucepan and bring to the boil, then add the cream and cayenne. If the flavour needs intensifying, simmer the soup to reduce it. Season with salt and pepper and serve in bowls topped with the garlic croutons.

smoked haddock chowder

Serves **4**
Preparation time **15 minutes**
Cooking time **30 minutes**

4 large, round **white bread
  rolls**
1 **egg**, lightly beaten
50 g (2 oz) **butter**
8 **spring onions** chopped
1 **garlic clove**, crushed
2 large, **waxy potatoes**,
  peeled and cut into cubes
350 ml (12 fl oz) **milk**
200 ml (7 fl oz) **double cream**
200 ml (7 fl oz) **Basic Fish
  Stock** (see page 15)
250 g (8 oz) **canned
  sweetcorn**, drained
500 g (1 lb) **smoked
  haddock**, skinned and cut
  into large chunks
1 tablespoon **olive oil**
8 **streaky bacon** rashers,
  chopped
2 tablespoons chopped
  parsley
salt and **pepper**

Cut the tops off the bread rolls and pull out the soft centre, leaving a bowl shape and a lid. Place on a baking sheet in a preheated oven, 160°C (325°F), Gas Mark 3, and bake for 25 minutes until they have dried out and become crispy. Brush the inside of the bread rolls with the egg. Place the rolls back in the oven for a further 5 minutes to dry out once again. Remove from the oven and set aside.

Heat the butter in a large saucepan. Add the spring onions and fry until soft. Add the garlic and potatoes and fry for a further minute. Pour in the milk, cream and stock and bring the soup to the boil, then reduce the heat and simmer for 10 minutes, or until the potatoes are almost cooked.

Add the sweetcorn and smoked haddock to the pan and simmer for a further 5 minutes until the fish has cooked. Season with salt and pepper.

Heat the oil in a frying pan and fry the bacon until crispy. When ready to serve, place the bread bowls in shallow bowls. Pour the soup into the bread bowls, then top with the bacon and a sprinkling of parsley.

For clam chowder, follow the recipe above but replace the smoked haddock with 1 kg (2 lb) cleaned clams (see page 12). Heat a saucepan over a high heat and add 100 ml (3½ fl oz) white wine. Tip in the clams, cover and steam until they open, discarding any that don't. Strain the clams and pick about half of the clams out of their shells. Add these to the soup with the sweetcorn, along with the clams that are still in their shells. Serve as above.

vegetable broth & sea bass

Serves **4**
Preparation time **5 minutes**
Cooking time **7–8 minutes**

750 ml (1 ¼ pints) good-quality
  chicken or **vegetable stock**
2 tablespoons **olive oil**
4 **sea bass fillets**, about
  200 g (7 oz) each, skin on,
  pin-boned
1 **fennel bulb**, cut into
  8, herby tops reserved
12 **fine asparagus spears**
150 g (5 oz) **frozen peas**,
  thawed
150 g (5 oz) **broad beans**,
  podded
small handful of **mint leaves**,
  torn
small handful of **basil leaves**,
  torn
salt and **pepper**

Bring the stock to the boil in a saucepan.

Heat the oil in a frying pan. Season the sea bass with salt and pepper and place, skin-side down, in the pan. Cook for 3–4 minutes until the skin is crispy, then turn the fish over and cook for 1 minute on the other side.

Meanwhile, place the fennel in the stock and simmer for 3 minutes, or until it is just starting to become tender. Add the asparagus, peas and broad beans to the pan and cook for a further 1–2 minutes. Season the broth with salt and pepper.

Divide the vegetable broth between 4 bowls and sprinkle with a few torn mint and basil leaves. Top the dish with the pan-fried sea bass and reserved herby fennel tops and serve.

For Thai broth with prawns, peel and devein 500 g (1 lb) raw tiger prawns, reserving the shells and heads. Heat 750 ml (1 ¼ pints) Basic Fish Stock (see page 15) or chicken stock in a saucepan. Add the prawn shells and heads, 2 roughly chopped lemon grass stalks, a 5 cm (2 inch) piece of fresh root ginger, 1 dried red chilli and 2 kaffir lime leaves. Allow the stock to infuse off the heat for 30 minutes. Strain the stock and return it to a clean saucepan. Add the prawns and poach for 3–4 minutes until cooked. Add 125 g (4 oz) sugar snap peas at the last minute.

tomato stew with clams & chorizo

Serves **4**
Preparation time **15 minutes**
Cooking time **20–25 minutes**

300 g (10 oz) **chorizo sausage**, cut into chunks
1 teaspoon **coriander seeds**, crushed
1 tablespoon **fennel seeds**, crushed
1 **onion**, finely chopped
1 **red chilli**, deseeded and finely chopped
2 **garlic cloves**, crushed
50 ml (2 fl oz) **white wine**
400 g (13 oz) can **chopped tomatoes**
200 ml (7 fl oz) **Basic Fish Stock** (see page 15)
500 g (1 lb) **clams**, cleaned (see page 12)
a few **basil leaves**, to garnish

Heat a large saucepan over a high heat. Add the chorizo and fry until the natural oil has been released and the chorizo is starting to colour. Remove the chorizo from the pan, leaving behind its oil, and set aside.

Fry the coriander and fennel seeds in the chorizo oil for 1 minute, then add the onion and chilli and fry until the onion has softened but not coloured. Add the garlic and fry for a further minute. Pour in the wine and leave to bubble until just 1 tablespoon of liquid is left. Add the tomatoes and stock, bring the stew to the boil and return the chorizo to the pan. Tip in the clams, then cover and cook until the clams have opened, discarding any that don't.

Divide the stew between 4 bowls, garnish with a few basil leaves and serve with crusty bread.

For spicy bean stew with pan-fried John Dory,

follow the recipe above but omit the clams and chorizo and add 400 g (13 oz) can haricot beans and 400 g (13 oz) can kidney beans, drained. Pan-fry the fillets of 2 John Dory and serve with the bean stew.

cuttlefish stew

Serves **4**
Preparation time **15 minutes**
Cooking time **1 hour
10 minutes**

2 tablespoons **olive oil**
1 **onion**, finely chopped
1 **fennel bulb**, finely chopped
2 **garlic cloves**, crushed
1 tablespoon **smoked paprika**
1 tablespoon **paprika**
2 tablespoons **tomato purée**
2 x 400 g (13 oz) cans
   chopped tomatoes
150 ml (¼ pint) **red wine**
1 kg (2 lb) **cuttlefish**, cleaned
   and cut into strips
400 g (13 oz) can **butter
   beans**, drained
1 teaspoon **caster sugar**
   (optional)
2 tablespoons finely chopped
   parsley

Heat the oil in a large saucepan. Add the onion and fennel and fry until the onion is soft but not coloured. Add the garlic, paprika and fry for a further minute. Add the tomato purée, tomatoes, wine and cuttlefish. Bring the stew to the boil, then reduce the heat, cover and simmer for 1 hour, or until the cuttlefish is tender. If the dish becomes a little dry, add some water or stock.

Add the butter beans and warm through. Taste and add the sugar if necessary. Finally, add the parsley and serve with warm crusty bread or Lemon and Parsley Mashed Potatoes (see below).

For lemon & parsley mashed potatoes, to serve as an accompaniment, peel 4 floury potatoes, cut into pieces and boil in lightly salted water until tender. Drain and mash the potatoes. Beat in 125 g (4 oz) butter and enough double cream to make a really creamy mash. Grate in the rind of 1 lemon and 2 tablespoons finely chopped parsley. Season to taste with salt and pepper.

prawn & pork wonton soup

Serves **4**
Preparation time **25 minutes**
Cooking time **5–6 minutes**

100 g (3½ oz) **minced pork**
150 g (5 oz) **raw peeled prawns**
4 **spring onions**, finely chopped
1 **garlic clove**
1 cm (½ inch) piece of **fresh root ginger**, peeled and chopped
1 tablespoon **oyster sauce**
20 **wonton wrappers**
750 ml (1¼ pints) **chicken stock**
1 head of **Chinese spring greens**, shredded
1–2 tablespoons **Thai fish sauce**

To serve
leaves from a small bunch of **coriander**
1 tablespoon **sesame seeds**
1 **lime**, cut into wedges (optional)

Place the pork, prawns, 2 of the spring onions, the garlic, ginger and oyster sauce in a food processor and blend to a paste.

Take 1 of the wonton wrappers and place 1 teaspoon of the prawn and pork mixture in the centre. Dampen the edges of the wrapper with a little water and bring them up around the filling, enclosing it completely in a little bundle. Repeat with the remainder of the wrappers and prawn and pork mixture.

Bring the stock to the boil in a large saucepan, then reduce the heat, add the wontons and simmer for 4–5 minutes. Remove 1 of the wontons and check that it has become firm, which will indicate that it is cooked.

Add the spring greens to the pan and cook for 1 minute. Season the stock with the fish sauce.

Divide the soup between 4 bowls and serve with a few coriander leaves, a sprinkling of sesame seeds and a lime wedge.

For sesame wontons with soy dipping sauce,

make the wontons as per the recipe above and steam them in a bamboo steamer for 5 minutes. Remove the wontons from the steamer and sprinkle over 2 tablespoons sesame seeds. Make a dipping sauce by mixing together 3 tablespoons light soy sauce, 2 teaspoons grated fresh root ginger, 1 finely sliced red chilli and 1 tablespoon Thai fish sauce.

thai coconut soup

Serves **4**
Preparation time **20 minutes**
Cooking time **15 minutes**

200 g (7 oz) **dried rice noodles**
3 tablespoons **vegetable oil**
2 **shallots**, very finely chopped
1 **green chilli**, deseeded and very finely chopped
2 **lemon grass stalks**, bottom two-thirds only, very finely chopped
5 cm (2 inch) piece of **fresh root ginger**, peeled and grated
400 ml (14 fl oz) can **coconut milk**
300 ml (½ pint) **chicken stock**
2 tablespoons **Thai fish sauce**
juice of 1½ **limes**
1 teaspoon **brown sugar**
400 g (13 oz) **monkfish tail**, cut into large chunks
250 g (8 oz) **mussels**, scrubbed and debearded (see page 12)
4 **red mullet fillets**, pin-boned
salt and **pepper**

Place the noodles in a heatproof bowl and cover with boiling water. Leave for 5 minutes, then drain.

Heat 2 tablespoons of the oil in a large saucepan. Add the shallots, chilli, lemon grass and ginger and fry over a gentle heat until the shallot has softened. Add the coconut milk and stock and bring to the boil, then reduce the heat and simmer for 5 minutes to infuse the flavours. Season the soup by adding the fish sauce, the juice of 1 lime and the sugar. Adjust quantities to taste.

Add the drained noodles and the monkfish to the soup and cook for 2 minutes. Discard any mussels that don't shut when tapped, then add to the soup. Cook until they open and the monkfish is firm.

Meanwhile, heat the remaining oil in a frying pan. Season the mullet with salt and pepper and fry, skin-side down, for 3 minutes, or until the skin becomes crispy. Turn the fish over and cook for a further minute. Squeeze the remaining lime juice over the fish.

Divide the soup between 4 bowls, removing any mussels that have not opened, and top with the mullet.

For mussels in saffron broth, sweat a finely chopped onion and 2 finely chopped garlic cloves in a little oil in a saucepan. Add a large glass of white wine, a pinch of saffron threads and 1.5 kg (3 lb) scrubbed and debearded mussels to the pan (first discarding any that don't shut when tapped), cover and cook until the mussels open (discarding any that don't), removing the lid and stirring once or twice during the cooking process. Add 200 ml (7 fl oz) double cream and a large handful of chopped parsley, stir well and season.

salads & starters

seared salmon with avocado salad

Serves **4**
Preparation time **15 minutes**
Cooking time **10–12 minutes**

2 tablespoons **olive oil**
4 pieces of **salmon fillet**,
    about 200 g (7 oz) each, skin
    on and pin-boned
1 large **orange**
2 tablespoons **extra virgin
    olive oil**
salt and **pepper**

Avocado salad

2 ripe **avocados**, peeled and
    cut into 1 cm (½ inch) dice
1 **red chilli**, deseeded and
    finely chopped
juice of 1 **lime**
1 tablespoon roughly chopped
    coriander
1 tablespoon **olive oil**

Heat a small frying pan over a high heat. When the pan
is hot, add the olive oil. Season the salmon with salt and
pepper and place it, skin-side down, in the pan. Cook
for 4 minutes, then turn the fish over and cook for a
further 2 minutes.

Heat another small frying pan on the hob. Cut the
orange in half and place the orange halves, cut-side
down, in the pan. Sear the orange halves until they
start to blacken. Remove the oranges from the pan
and squeeze the juice into the frying pan. Bring the
juice to the boil and reduce it until you have around
1 tablespoon left. Whisk in the extra virgin olive oil and
season with salt and pepper.

Place the avocados in a mixing bowl, add the remaining
ingredients and season with salt and pepper.

Spoon the avocado salad into the centre of each plate.
Place a piece of salmon on top and drizzle with the
burnt orange vinaigrette.

For salmon with orange couscous, pan-fry 4 salmon
steaks as above. Bring 400 ml (14 fl oz) freshly
squeezed orange juice to the boil in a saucepan with
2 tablespoons raisins. Place 300 g (10 oz) couscous
in a heatproof bowl and pour over the orange juice.
Cover the bowl with clingfilm and allow the couscous
to steam for 5 minutes before fluffing the grains up
with a fork. Add 1 tablespoon olive oil, a large handful
of chopped coriander and 2 tablespoons pine nuts.
Serve with crème fraîche and the warm salmon.

plaice with fennel salad

Serves **4**
Preparation time **20 minutes**
Cooking time **5–10 minutes**

Salad
1 **fennel bulb**, finely sliced
200 g (7 oz) **frozen peas**,
  thawed
200 g (7 oz) podded **broad
  beans**
5 **radishes**, finely sliced
75 g (3 oz) **watercress**

Dressing
1 tablespoon **wholegrain
  mustard**
1 teaspoon **clear honey**
1 tablespoon **white wine
  vinegar**
3 tablespoons **olive oil**
salt and **pepper**

Fish
2 tablespoons **olive oil**
4 **plaice fillets**, skin on and
  pin-boned
2 tablespoons **plain flour**,
  seasoned wth salt and
  pepper
1 **lemon**

Place the fennel in a bowl along with the peas, broad beans, radishes and watercress.

Make the dressing by mixing together the mustard, honey, vinegar and oil. Season to taste with salt and pepper. Add enough of the dressing to the salad to coat all the ingredients. Set aside while you cook the plaice.

Heat a little of the oil in a very hot frying pan and dust the plaice fillets with the seasoned flour. Place the fish, skin-side down, in the pan. Cook for 3 minutes on the skin side, then carefully turn the fish over and cook for a further 2 minutes. (Depending on the size of your pan, you may need to cook the fish in 2 batches.) Once the fish is cooked, squeeze a little lemon juice over the fish and serve with the fennel salad.

For hot honey & mustard salmon, mix together 1 heaped tablespoon wholegrain mustard and 2 tablespoons clear honey. Pour over 4 skinless salmon fillets and place in a preheated oven, 180°C (350°F), Gas Mark 4, for about 8–10 minutes or until cooked. Serve with buttered new potatoes.

mackerel with baked beetroot

Serves **4**
Preparation time **15 minutes**
Cooking time **1 hour**
  5 minutes

4 small **mackerel**, filleted
1 tablespoon **olive oil**
salt and **pepper**

Beetroot
2 large **raw beetroot**
2 **garlic cloves**, sliced
4 **thyme sprigs**
2 tablespoons **olive oil**, plus
  extra for drizzling

Horseradish Cream
  (optional)
150 ml (¼ pint) **crème fraîche**
2 tablespoons **mayonnaise**
2 tablespoons finely chopped
  chives
1–2 tablespoons **creamed**
  horseradish

Wash the beetroot well. Wrap the beetroot in a foil parcel with the garlic, thyme, salt and pepper to taste and oil. Place in a preheated oven, 180°C (350°F), Gas Mark 4, for around 1 hour until the beetroot is cooked and a knife can easily be inserted into the centre. Once cool enough to handle, peel the beetroot. Cut into bite-sized pieces, drizzle with a little oil and season with salt and pepper. Set aside.

Mix together all the horseradish cream ingredients, if using, and season with salt and pepper.

Place the fish on a nonstick baking sheet, skin-side up. Brush the skin with the oil and season with salt and pepper. Cook under a preheated grill on this side until the skin is crispy, about 3 minutes, then carefully turn over and cook for a further 2 minutes on the other side.

Serve the mackerel with the roasted beetroot and horseradish cream, if using.

For smoked mackerel pâté, place 300 g (10 oz) skinless smoked mackerel in a food processor with 3 tablespoons crème fraiche and 2 tablespoons horseradish sauce. Blend until smooth, then fold in lemon juice to taste and season with salt and pepper. Serve with toast.

devilled oysters

Serves **4**
Preparation time **25 minutes**
Cooking time **15 minutes**

12 **oysters**
1 teaspoon **mustard seeds**
75 g (3 oz) **butter**
2 **shallots**, finely chopped
½ **celery stick**, finely chopped
1 **garlic clove**, crushed
1 tablespoon **white wine
   vinegar**
1 teaspoon **Tabasco sauce**
1 tablespoon chopped **chives**
1 tablespoon chopped **flat
   leaf parsley**
plenty of **sea salt** and **pepper**

Hold an oyster, wrapped in a heavyweight cloth, with the rounded shell underneath. Push a strong knife, preferably an oyster knife, into the small gap at the hinged end. Twist the knife to sever the muscle and separate the shells.

Discard the top shell. Run the blade of the knife under the oyster to loosen it, holding the shell steady to prevent the juices from running out. Place the oyster in a grill pan, lined with a layer of salt to keep the shells from flopping over, and repeat with the remainder.

Dry-fry the mustard seeds in a frying pan until they start to pop. Add the butter, the shallots and celery and fry for 3 minutes. Add the garlic and a little salt and pepper and fry for a further 2 minutes. Stir in the vinegar, Tabasco sauce and two-thirds of each herb.

Spoon the mixture over the oysters and cook under a preheated grill for 5–8 minutes, or until the oysters are just firm. Serve scattered with the remaining herbs.

For oysters with Bloody Mary dressing, open the oysters as above. Pour their natural juices into a small bowl and place on a serving platter lined with sea salt. Mix 6 tablespoons tomato juice with the oyster juices. Add a squeeze of lemon juice and a dash each of Tabasco and Worcestershire sauce. Stir well and taste for seasoning. Pour a little of the tomato mixture into each of the oyster shells, then sprinkle with a little celery salt. Serve immediately.

cod with roasted tomato toast

Serves **4**
Preparation time **15 minutes**
Cooking time 1¼ **hours**

4 ripe **tomatoes**, halved
a few **thyme sprigs**
2 tablespoons **olive oil**
4 **cod fillets**, about 200 g
   (7 oz) each, skin on and pin-
   boned
4 slices of **ciabatta**
1 **garlic clove**
salt and **pepper**

Dressing
large handful of **basil**
4 tablespoons **olive oil**
2 tablespoons freshly grated
   Parmesan cheese, plus
   some shavings to garnish
   (optional)

Place the tomatoes on a baking sheet, season with salt and pepper, sprinkle with the thyme sprigs and drizzle with 1 tablespoon of the oil. Roast in a preheated oven, 160°C (325°F), Gas Mark 3, for 1 hour until soft, then turn the oven up to 180°C (350°F), Gas Mark 4. Season the cod and roast along with the tomatoes in the oven for 10–12 minutes, or until the fish is cooked and the tomatoes have softened.

Brush both sides of the bread with the remaining oil. Preheat a griddle pan and griddle the bread until golden brown on both sides. Then rub both sides with the garlic clove.

Place the ingredients for the dressing in a small food processor and blend until smooth. You can also do this using a hand blender.

Top the toast with the tomatoes and then serve with the cod. Drizzle a little of the dressing over the top and garnish with some Parmesan shavings.

For roasted cod & tomato pasta, while the tomatoes and cod are roasting as above, cook 300 g (10 oz) dried pasta according to the instructions on the packet, then drain. Cut the roasted tomatoes into small pieces and flake the cod. Stir through the warm pasta with some of the dressing, prepared as above.

crispy salt cod & chorizo salad

Serves **4**

Preparation time **15 minutes**, plus soaking

Cooking time **20 minutes**

500 g (1 lb) piece of **salt cod**

225 g (7½ oz) **chorizo sausage**, sliced

1 **red pepper**, cored, deseeded and finely sliced

3 large handfuls of **mixed salad leaves**

3 **spring onions**, finely sliced

200 g (7 oz) **frozen peas**, thawed

1 **celery stick**, finely sliced

Dressing

1 tablespoon **wholegrain mustard**

1 teaspoon **clear honey**

4 tablespoons **olive oil**

1 tablespoon **lemon juice**

salt and **pepper**

Soak the salt cod in cold water for at least 8 hours, changing the water as often as possible. Place the soaked salt cod in a saucepan and cover with fresh cold water. Bring to the boil, then reduce the heat and simmer for 5 minutes. Remove the fish and, when cool enough to handle, flake it into large chunks, removing any bones and skin. Set aside.

Heat a large frying pan over a medium heat. Add the chorizo and cook for 2 minutes, allowing it to brown. Turn the chorizo slices over and add the salt cod to the pan. Allow both the cod and chorizo to cook until crispy. Remove from the pan using a slotted spoon, leaving behind the excess fat from the chorizo. Fry the red pepper in the chorizo oil for 2 minutes. Remove from the pan.

Mix together the salad leaves, spring onions, peas and celery.

Whisk together the dressing ingredients. Add enough of the dressing to coat the salad leaves.

Place the dressed salad on a serving plate and top with the crispy chorizo, salt cod and red pepper.

For salt cod salad with chickpeas, rocket & tomato, soak the fish as above, then cut into 5 cm (2 inch) chunks. Heat 1 tablespoon olive oil in a frying pan. Add 300 g (10 oz) halved cherry tomatoes and 1 crushed garlic clove. Cook until softened and starting to break down. Add a 400 g (13 oz) can chickpeas, drained, and 2 handfuls of rocket leaves. Season with salt and pepper. Heat a little more olive oil in another frying pan and fry the cod until crispy. Stir through the tomatoes and chickpeas. Serve with crusty bread.

salmon & watercress roulade

Serves **4–6**
Preparation time **30 minutes**,
  plus cooling and chilling
Cooking time **25–30 minutes**

40 g (1 ½ oz) **butter**
40 g (1 ½ oz) **plain flour**
250 ml (8 fl oz) **milk**
4 **eggs**, separated
75 g (3 oz) **watercress**,
  roughly chopped, plus a few
  extra leaves to garnish
grated rind of 1 **lime**
3 tablespoons freshly grated
  Parmesan cheese
salt and **pepper**
lime wedges, to garnish
  (optional)

Filling

300 g (10 oz) **salmon fillet**,
  pin-boned and halved
200 ml (7 fl oz) **crème fraîche**
2 tablespoons freshly
  squeezed **lime juice**
salt and **pepper**

Line a 23 x 30 cm (9 x 12 inch) roasting tin with nonstick baking paper.

Melt the butter in a saucepan, stir in the flour and cook for 1 minute. Gradually mix in the milk and bring to the boil, stirring until thickened and smooth. Remove from the heat and stir in the egg yolks, watercress, lime rind and salt and pepper. Leave to cool for 15 minutes.

Whisk the egg whites into stiff peaks. Fold a large spoonful into the cooled sauce to loosen the mixture, then fold in the remaining egg whites. Spoon the mixture into the prepared tin and ease into the corners.

Bake the roulade in a preheated oven, 180°C (350°F), Gas Mark 4, for 15–20 minutes until it is well risen, golden brown and the top feels spongy. Cover with a clean tea towel and leave to cool for at least 1 hour.

Meanwhile, steam the salmon for 8–10 minutes until it is cooked. Leave to cool, before skinning, flaking and discarding any bones. Beat the crème fraîche with the lime juice and plenty of salt and pepper.

Place a large piece of baking paper on the work surface so that a short edge is nearest to you and sprinkle with the Parmesan. Turn the cooled roulade out on to the paper, remove the tin and peel away the lining paper.

Spread the roulade with the crème fraîche mixture, then the salmon. Roll up the roulade, starting from the shortest side nearest to you, using the paper to help. Place in the refrigerator for a least 30 minutes, then cut into thick slices and serve garnished with a few watercress leaves and lime wedges, if liked.

mackerel & wild rice niçoise

Serves **3–4**

Preparation time **20 minutes**, plus cooling

Cooking time **25 minutes**

100 g (3½ oz) **wild rice**

150 g (5 oz) **green beans**, halved

300 g (10 oz) large **mackerel fillets**, pin-boned

6 tablespoons **olive oil**

12 **black olives**

8 canned **anchovy fillets**, drained and halved

250 g (8 oz) **cherry tomatoes**, halved

3 **hard-boiled eggs**, cut into quarters

1 tablespoon **lemon juice**

1 tablespoon **French mustard**

2 tablespoons **chopped chives**

salt and **pepper**

Cook the rice in plenty of boiling water for 20–25 minutes, or until it is tender. (The grains will start to split open when they're just cooked.) Add the green beans and cook for 2 minutes.

Meanwhile, lay the mackerel on a foil-lined grill rack and brush with 1 tablespoon of the oil. Cook under a preheated grill for 8–10 minutes, or until cooked through. Leave to cool.

Drain the rice and beans and mix together in a salad bowl with the olives, anchovies, tomatoes and eggs. Flake the mackerel, discarding any stray bones, and add to the bowl.

Mix the remaining oil with the lemon juice, mustard, chives and a little salt and pepper, and add to the bowl. Toss the ingredients lightly together, cover and chill until ready to serve.

For fresh tuna & wild rice niçoise, replace the mackerel with 4 x 200 g (7 oz) fresh tuna steaks, frying them in a little olive oil for 2–3 minutes on each side so that they are just pink in the centre. Complete the recipe as above.

tuna pâté with toasted sourdough

Serves **4**

Preparation time **10 minutes**

Cooking time **5 minutes**

2 x 185 g (6½ oz) cans **tuna in brine**

3 tablespoons **mayonnaise**

1 tablespoon **tomato ketchup**

2 tablespoons **lemon juice**

1 tablespoon chopped **parsley**

1 **sourdough loaf**, thinly sliced

50 g (2 oz) **butter**

1 tablespoon **olive oil**

1 tablespoon **balsamic vinegar**

75 g (3 oz) **rocket leaves**, washed and drained

2 tablespoons roughly chopped **capers**

10 **sun-blushed tomatoes**, halved

10 **pitted black olives**, halved

salt and **pepper**

Drain the tuna and place it in a small food processor along with the mayonnaise, tomato ketchup and lemon juice. Blend until smooth, then stir in the parsley and season with salt and pepper. Alternatively, you can make this by hand just mixing the ingredients together. Spoon the pâté into individual pots.

Place the sourdough slices in a preheated griddle pan to toast or under a preheated grill. Spread with butter.

Mix together the oil and vinegar and lightly dress the rocket leaves. Toss in the capers, sun-blushed tomatoes and olives.

Serve a pot of the tuna pâté along with the warm buttered toast and rocket salad.

For seared tuna with sun-blushed tomato & olive salsa, season and lightly brush 4 fresh tuna steaks with olive oil. Sear them in a hot griddle pan for 2–3 minutes on each side. Mix together 20 sun-blushed tomatoes and 20 halved pitted black olives with 1 tablespoon baby capers, 1 tablespoon balsamic vinegar and 2 tablespoons olive oil. Season with salt and pepper and serve with the seared tuna.

grey mullet with pancetta salad

Serves **4**

Preparation time **8 minutes**

Cooking time **10–12 minutes**

4 **grey mullet fillets**, about
175 g (6 oz) each, skin on
and pin-boned

1 tablespoon **olive oil**

200 g (7 oz) **pancetta** or
streaky bacon, cubed

200 g (7 oz) **frozen peas**,
thawed

2 **baby gem lettuces**, outer
few leaves removed and cut
into 6

a few **thyme sprigs**

50 ml (2 fl oz) **white wine** or
water

20 g (¾ oz) **butter**

Season the fish and steam in a steamer for 4–5 minutes or until the fish has turned opaque.

Heat a frying pan over a high heat and add the olive oil. Fry the pancetta or bacon until crispy, then remove from the pan and set aside.

Place the peas, baby gem, thyme and wine in the frying pan and bring the pan up to a low simmer until the baby gem has softened slighty. Stir in the butter and season with salt and pepper.

Divide the pea mixture between 4 shallow bowls and top with the steamed grey mullet and a sprinkle of crispy pancetta or bacon.

For baby gem lettuce broth, add 500 ml (17 fl oz) chicken stock or Basic Fish Stock (see page 15) to the pan with the peas, baby gem and wine. Finish the dish with a sprinkle of chopped mint. Serve with crusty bread.

tuna with green beans & broccoli

Serves **4**

Preparation time **8 minutes**

Cooking time **15 minutes**

500 g (1 lb) **new potatoes**

250 g (8 oz) **fine green beans**, topped and tailed

200 g (7 oz) **tenderstem broccoli**

4 **fresh tuna steaks**, about 175 g (6 oz) each

1 tablespoon **olive oil**

50 g (2 oz) **toasted hazelnuts**, roughly chopped

salt and **pepper**

Dressing

4 tablespoons **hazelnut oil**

1 tablespoon **lemon juice**

1 teaspoon **Dijon mustard**

Cook the potatoes, beans and broccoli in lightly salted water until tender but still with a slight bite to them. Then plunge into ice-cold water to stop the cooking process. Drain and cut the potatoes into quarters lengthways.

Mix all the dressing ingredients together and season with salt and pepper.

Heat a griddle pan over a very high heat. Season the steaks and rub with oil. Place in the pan and sear on 1 side for about 1 minute, then turn over and sear again for a further minute (or longer if you want your tuna cooked through rather than pink).

Toss the potatoes, beans and broccoli in the dressing. Sprinkle with the hazelnuts and serve with the tuna.

For Asian green beans, to serve as an alternative accompaniment, mix together 1 tablespoon sesame oil, 2 teaspoons light soy sauce, 1 deseeded and finely chopped chilli, 1 teaspoon clear honey and 1 tablespoon chopped coriander. Cook 500 g (1 lb) topped and tailed green beans in salted boiling water, as above. Drain the beans and, while still warm, toss the dressing with the beans.

salmon with asian coleslaw

Serves **4**
Preparation time **20–25
minutes,** plus chilling
Cooking time **5 minutes**

1 tablespoon **coriander seeds**
1 tablespoon **cumin seeds**
500 g (1 lb) **thick salmon
fillet,** pin-boned and skinned
1 tablespoon **olive oil**
200 g (7 oz) **white cabbage,**
finely shredded
200 g (7 oz) **carrot,** grated
handful of **sugarsnap peas,**
sliced into 3 pieces on a
sharp angle
1 **green chilli,** deseeded and
finely chopped
handful of **coriander leaves**
50 g (2 oz) **roasted cashew
nuts,** roughly chopped
(optional)
sea salt and **pepper**

Dressing
juice of 2 **limes**
1 tablespoon **sesame oil**
2 teaspoons **palm sugar** or
brown sugar
1 teaspoon **light soy sauce**
1 tablespoon **Thai fish sauce**

Place the coriander and cumin seeds in small frying
pan and toast over a medium heat for a few minutes
until fragrant, taking care not to burn them. Lightly
crush the spices with a little sea salt and pepper in a
pestle and mortar. Rub the spices all over the salmon.

Heat the olive oil in a frying pan until smoking. Quickly
sear the salmon for 20 seconds on all sides. Remove
from the pan and place in the freezer for 20 minutes.

Mix all the dressing ingredients together.

Mix together the cabbage, carrot, sugar snap peas,
chilli and coriander leaves in a large mixing bowl.
Add enough of the dressing to coat all the vegetables.

Slice the salmon thinly with a very sharp knife. Cover
the base of a large platter with the salmon, pile the
Asian coleslaw in the centre of the plate or in a side
bowl and scatter with the cashew nuts, if liked.

For Indian-style coleslaw, mix together 200 g (7 oz)
shredded white cabbage, 200 g (7 oz) grated carrot,
1 tablespoon mint sauce and 100 ml (3½ fl oz)
natural yogurt. Season well and sprinkle with a few
toasted walnuts. Serve with pan-fried white fish such
as red mullet.

scallops with morcilla

Serves **6**

Preparation time **10 minutes**

Cooking time **5 minutes**

6 cleaned **king scallops,**
  preferably in their shells

25 g (1 oz) **morcilla sausage**

2 tablespoons **olive oil**

1 **spring onion**, finely sliced

1 teaspoon chopped **lemon thyme**

salt and **pepper**

Pat the scallops dry on kitchen paper and season lightly with salt and pepper. Finely chop or break the morcilla into small pieces.

Heat the oil in a small frying pan and gently fry the scallops for 1 minute on each side. Transfer them to the cleaned shells or to small, warm serving dishes if the scallops were ready-shelled.

Add the spring onion, lemon thyme and morcilla to the pan and heat gently, stirring, for 1 minute. Season lightly with salt and pepper and spoon over the scallops with the cooking juices to serve.

For coriander dressing, to serve as an accompaniment, whiz 150 ml (¼ pint) thick Greek yogurt with 1 green chilli and a large bunch of coriander in a small food processor. Season with salt and pepper to taste, then spoon over the scallops and morcilla.

baked arbroath smokie soufflés

Serves **4**

Preparation time **10 minutes**, plus cooling

Cooking time **30 minutes**

30 g (1¼ oz) **butter**, plus extra for greasing

30 g (1¼ oz) **plain flour**

150 ml (¼ pint) **milk**

2 **eggs**, separated

150 g (5 oz) **Arbroath Smokies** or **cooked smoked haddock**, flaked, plus 50 g (2 oz) extra to garnish (optional)

150 ml (¼ pint) **double cream**

salt and **pepper**

Lemon Hollandaise Sauce, to serve (see below)

Melt the butter in a saucepan over a low heat, add the flour and stir continuously for 1 minute. Remove from the heat and gradually add the milk, whisking until smooth. Return the pan to a low heat and bring to the boil, stirring continuously, then reduce the heat and simmer for a further minute. Allow it to cool slightly before beating in the egg yolks. Fold in the flaked fish.

Whisk the egg whites until they form firm peaks, then fold them into the fish mixture. Gently spoon the mixture into 4 lightly buttered ramekins or moulds (fill them about three-quarters full). Place the filled moulds in a roasting pan and fill this with boiling water until it comes one-third of the way up the sides of the ramekins. Bake in a preheated oven, 180°C (350°F), Gas Mark 4, for 12–15 minutes, or until set, then remove from the oven and the water and leave to cool.

Unmould the soufflés and place in either individual serving dishes or 1 large dish. Pour over the cream and return to the oven for a further 10 minutes until hot.

Top with a little more flaked fish before serving with some Lemon Hollandaise Sauce (see below).

For lemon hollandaise sauce, to serve as an accompaniment, melt 200 g (7 oz) butter in a small saucepan. Place 2 egg yolks and the rind of 1 lemon in a food processor. When the butter is about to boil, turn the food processor on and pour the butter in through the funnel in a steady stream. When all the butter has been incorporated, turn the processor off, add about 2 tablespoons lemon juice and season with salt and pepper. Blend once more and serve immediately.

thai-style crab cakes with salsa

Serves **4**
Preparation time **20 minutes**
Cooking time **8 minutes**

625 g (1¼ lb) **fresh white crabmeat**
400 g (13 oz) **floury potatoes**, cooked and mashed
2.5 cm (1 inch) piece of **fresh root ginger**, peeled and finely grated
grated rind of **1 lime**
1 **red chilli**, deseeded and finely chopped
1 tablespoon **mayonnaise**
5 tablespoons **vegetable oil**, for shallow-frying

Salsa
400 g (13 oz) can **black-eyed beans**, drained
1 **red pepper**, cored, deseeded and finely diced
300 g (10 oz) can **sweetcorn**, drained
3 tablespoons **lime juice**
2 tablespoons **olive oil**
2 tablespoons chopped **coriander**
salt and **pepper**

Mix together the crab, mashed potatoes, ginger, lime rind, chilli and mayonnaise. Season the mixture well with salt and pepper. Divide the mixture into 12 portions and shape into cakes with your hands.

Heat the vegetable oil in a frying pan and fry the crab cakes for 3–4 minutes on each side until they are golden brown.

Make the salsa by mixing together the black-eyed beans, red pepper and sweetcorn. Squeeze over the lime juice and stir in the olive oil. Season with salt and pepper. Finally, mix in the chopped coriander.

For salmon & lemon fish cakes, mix together 400 g (13 oz) cooked and mashed floury potatoes and 400 g (13 oz) poached and flaked salmon fillet along with the grated rind of 2 lemons and 1 tablespoon mayonnaise. Season well with salt and pepper. Shape the mixture into cakes as above and fry in a little olive oil until crispy.

mackerel & asparagus tart

Serves **4**

Preparation time **20 minutes**, plus chilling

Cooking time **30–35 minutes**

8 **asparagus spears**, trimmed and blanched

250 g (8 oz) **smoked mackerel**, skinned

2 **eggs**

100 ml (3½ fl oz) **milk**

salt and **pepper**

100 ml (3½ fl oz) **double cream**

Pastry

200 g (7 oz) **plain flour**, plus extra for dusting

75 g (3 oz) **lightly salted butter**, chilled and diced

1 **egg**, plus 1 **egg yolk**

Put the flour, butter, egg and egg yolk in a food processor and blend until a soft dough is formed. If the pastry won't come together, add a drop of cold water. Take the dough out of the processor and knead lightly for 1 minute until it is smooth. Place it in a freezer bag or wrap in clingfilm and chill in the refrigerator for at least 30 minutes. Alternatively, make the pastry by hand by rubbing the butter into the flour until it resembles breadcrumbs, then working in the eggs.

Roll the pastry out on a well-floured work surface until it is about 3 mm (⅛ inch) thick and line a 25 cm (10 inch) round, fluted tart tin. Trim off the excess pastry. Chill the lined tart tin for 1 hour.

Line the tart with a piece of nonstick baking paper, cover with baking beans, then place in a preheated oven, 180°C (350°F), Gas Mark 4, for 10–12 minutes until lightly golden. Remove from the oven and take away the baking paper and beans. Place back in the oven for a further 2 minutes to dry out the base of the pastry case. Remove from the oven.

Slice each asparagus spear into 3 on the angle. Flake the fish into the pastry case and add the asparagus. Mix together the eggs, milk and cream. Season with salt and pepper. Pour the mixture into the pastry case and cook it in the oven for 20–25 minutes until the mixture has set.

For smoked salmon & pea tart, follow the recipe as above but replace the smoked mackerel and asparagus with 400 g (13 oz) shredded smoked salmon, 200 g (7 oz) thawed frozen peas and 2 tablespoons chopped dill. Season with pepper only.

sea bass with sauce vierge

Serves **4**
Preparation time **20 minutes**
Cooking time **5 minutes**

1 tablespoon **olive oil**
4 **sea bass fillets**, about
175 g (6 oz) each, skin on
and pin-boned
rocket leaves
salt and **pepper**

Sauce
4 ripe **tomatoes**, skinned,
deseeded and finely diced
1 **shallot**, finely diced
2 tablespoons **olive oil**
squeeze of **lemon juice**
a few **basil leaves**, shredded

Mix together the tomatoes and shallot. Add the oil and stir gently to combine. Add enough lemon juice, salt and pepper to taste. At the last minute before serving, add the basil leaves.

Heat the oil in a frying pan over a high heat. Season the sea bass with salt and pepper. When the pan is hot, fry the fish, skin-side down, for 3–4 minutes until the skin is golden brown and crispy. Turn the fish over and cook for a further minute. Remove from the pan and serve with the sauce vierge and rocket leaves.

For salsa verde, as an alternative to the sauce vierge, mix together 5 tablespoons chopped parsley leaves, 1 tablespoon chopped basil leaves, 2 tablespoons chopped mint leaves, 1 teaspoon Dijon mustard, 3 finely chopped canned anchovy fillets, 1 teaspoon chopped capers and 1 crushed garlic clove. Stir in 100 ml (3½ fl oz) olive oil. Season to taste and serve with pan-fried sea bass or any other fish.

squid with lemon & caper dressing

Serves **4**

Preparation time **10 minutes**,
  plus marinating

Cooking time **5 minutes**

8 small or 4 large **squid**,
  cleaned (see page 12) and
  halved lengthways, tentacles
  discarded

2 tablespoons **olive oil**

1 teaspoon **ground cumin**

grated rind and juice of
  1 lemon

50 ml (2 fl oz) **white wine**

2 tablespoons **capers**

salt and **pepper**

Open the squid out and pat dry with kitchen paper.
Lay them on a chopping board, shiny-side down,
and, using a sharp knife, lightly score a fine diamond
pattern on the flesh, being careful not to cut all the way
through. Place the squid in a non-metallic bowl along
with the oil, cumin, lemon rind, half the lemon juice
and a little pepper (no salt at this stage). Leave in the
refrigerator to marinate for at least 30 minutes, but
better still overnight.

Heat a frying pan until it is very hot. Add the squid to
the pan in batches, scored-side down, and cook for
about 1–2 minutes, or until it turns white and loses its
transparency. Remove from the pan and keep warm
while cooking the rest of the squid.

Return the pan to the heat and deglaze the pan with
the wine. Allow the wine to boil for a minute to burn off
the alcohol. Remove the pan from the heat and add the
remaining lemon juice and finally the capers. Season
the squid with salt and pepper and serve with the pan
juices poured over.

For mixed herb salad, to serve as an accompaniment,
mix together a large handful of parsley leaves with
a small handful each of mint and coriander leaves
in a salad bowl. In another bowl, mix together 2
tablespoons lemon juice, 2 tablespoons olive oil
and 1 crushed garlic clove. Pour the dressing over
the herb salad.

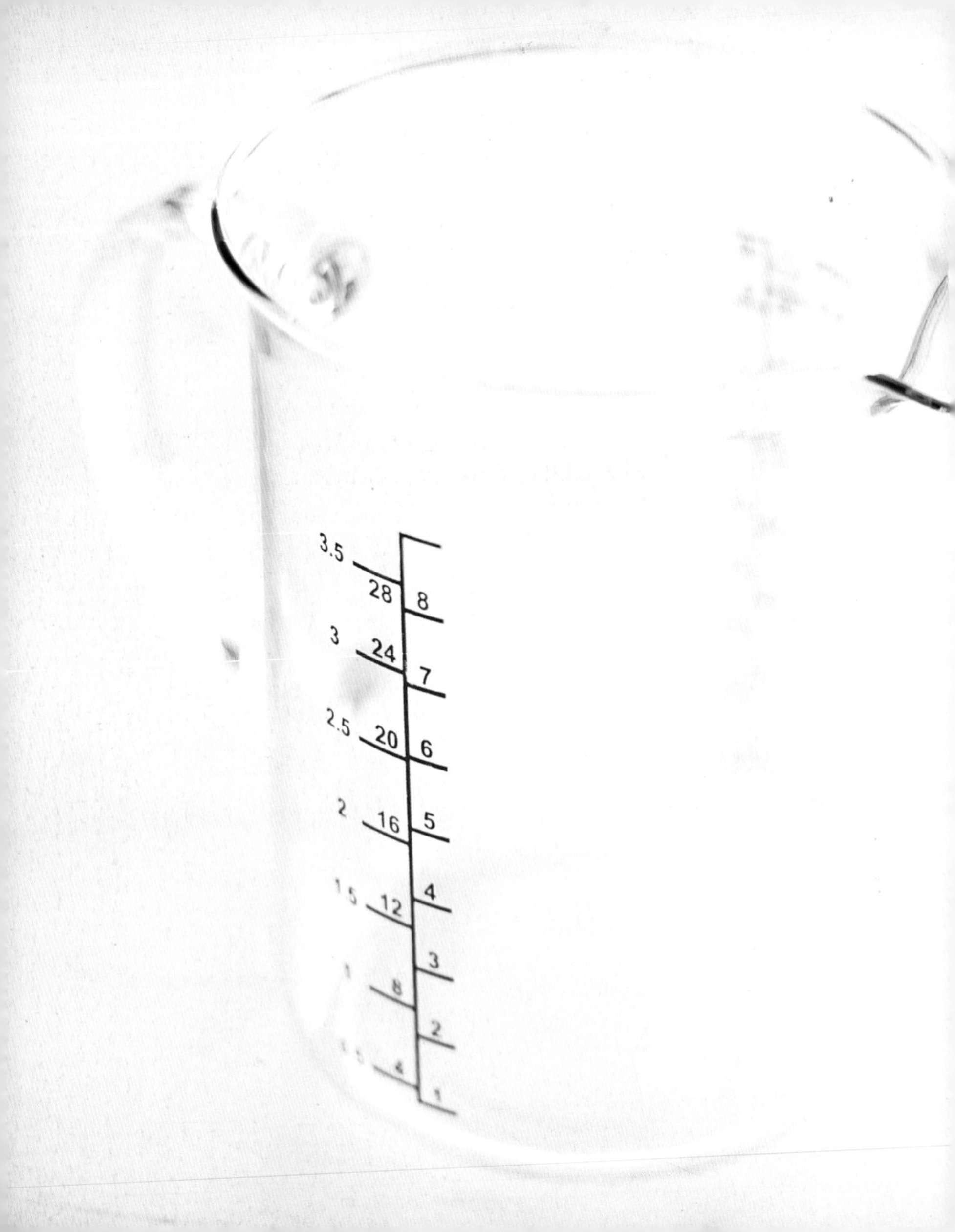
3.5
28
8
3
24
7
2.5
20
6
2
16
5
12
4
3
8
2
1

pastas, pulses & grains

kedgeree with soft-poached eggs

Serves **4**
Preparation time **5 minutes**
Cooking time **18–20 minutes**

50 g (2 oz) **butter**
6 **spring onions**, chopped
2 tablespoons **mild curry powder**
300 g (10 oz) **basmati rice**
300 ml (10 fl oz) **chicken stock**
250 g (8 oz) **smoked haddock**, skinned and cut into chunks
200 ml (7 fl oz) **whipping cream**
3 tablespoons chopped **parsley**
1 tablespoon **white wine vinegar** or **malt vinegar**
4 very fresh large **eggs**
1 **lemon**, cut into wedges
salt and **pepper**
mango chutney, to serve

Melt the butter in a large saucepan over a medium heat. Add the spring onions and fry until soft. Add the curry powder and fry for a further minute until fragrant. Add the rice to the pan and stir well.

Pour in the stock and bring to the boil, then simmer for 7–10 minutes, or until the rice is just cooked. Add the smoked haddock, cream and parsley. Cook for a further 2 minutes until the fish is cooked and firm. Season with salt and pepper.

Bring a large saucepan of water to the boil. Add the vinegar and a pinch of salt. Whisk the water around the pan, then crack the first egg into the centre of the spiral of water. Reduce the heat and simmer for 2–3 minutes until the white of the egg is set but the yolk is still soft. Remove from the pan using a slotted spoon and plunge into a bowl of ice-cold water to stop the cooking process. Repeat with the remaining eggs. Once all the eggs are cooked, bring the water back up to the simmer and return the eggs to the water for 1 minute to warm through.

Serve the hot kedgeree with the poached eggs, a wedge of lemon and some mango chutney.

For homemade mango chutney, to serve as an accompaniment, heat 125 ml (4 fl oz) white wine vinegar and 200 g (7 oz) caster sugar in a saucepan until the sugar dissolves. Add the peeled and diced flesh of 2 mangoes, ½ deseeded and finely chopped red chilli, 1 crushed garlic clove and 4 tablespoons lemon juice. Bring to the boil, then reduce the heat and simmer for 30 minutes until it is a jammy consistency. Pour into sterilized jars and seal tightly.

scallops with spiced lentils

Serves **4**

Preparation time **10 minutes**

Cooking time **20–25 minutes**

250 g (8 oz) **split red lentils**

5 tablespoons **olive oil**

25 g (1 oz) **butter**

1 **onion**, finely chopped

1 **aubergine**, cut into 1 cm
  (½ inch) cubes

1 **garlic clove**, crushed

1 tablespoon **curry powder**

1 tablespoon chopped **parsley**

12 cleaned **king scallops**,
  corals removed (optional)

4 tablespoons **Greek yogurt**

salt and **pepper**

Cook the lentils in water according to the instructions on the packet. Drain and set aside.

Heat 1 tablespoon of the oil and the butter in a frying pan over a medium heat. Add the onion and cook slowly until golden brown, about 10 minutes. When the onion has browned, remove it from the pan and turn the heat up to high. Add another 2 tablespoons of the oil to the pan and fry the aubergine in batches until coloured and softened.

Return the onion to the pan along with the garlic, curry powder and cooked lentils. Fry for a further minute to warm everything through. Season with salt and pepper and finally stir in the parsley.

Heat a frying pan over a high heat and add the remaining oil. Season the scallops with salt and pepper. Place them in the frying pan and cook for 1 minute on each side.

Serve the scallops immediately with the spiced lentils and Greek yogurt.

For scallops with dhal & spinach, cook 250 g (8 oz) yellow split pea lentils according to the instructions on the packet. Drain the lentils and set aside. Fry 1 finely chopped onion in a little vegetable oil with 1 crushed garlic clove. Add 1 teaspoon curry powder, 1 teaspoon garam masala and a pinch of turmeric to the pan and fry for 1 minute. Add the lentils with a little water or chicken stock to moisten the mixture. Add 500 g (1 lb) washed baby spinach and stir through until wilted. Cook the scallops as above with a light sprinkle of curry powder on each. Serve with the dhal.

prawn, courgette & pea risotto

Serves **4**
Preparation time **10 minutes**
Cooking time **25–30 minutes**

2 tablespoons **olive oil**
1 small **onion**, finely chopped
1 **garlic clove**, crushed
375 g (12 oz) **risotto rice**
250 ml (8 fl oz) **white wine**
about 1.5 litres (2½ pints) hot **chicken stock** or **Basic Fish Stock** (see page 15)
20 **large raw peeled prawns**
1 large or 2 small **courgettes**, cut into thin discs
200 g (7 oz) **peas**, thawed if frozen or blanched if fresh
125 g (4 oz) **butter**
2 tablespoons chopped **mint**
grated rind of 1 **lemon** and juice of ½ lemon
salt and **pepper**

Heat the oil in a frying pan, add the onion and fry until translucent. Add the garlic and risotto rice and fry for 2 minutes, stirring to coat the rice with the oil. Pour in the wine and leave to bubble until just 1 tablespoon of liquid is left.

Add the stock over a medium heat, a ladleful at a time, stirring continuously. Allow each ladleful of stock to be absorbed before adding the next. Keep adding stock until the rice is cooked but still has a slight bite to it. This should take about 15–20 minutes.

Add the prawns and courgettes just before the last couple of ladles of stock go in. Cook until the prawns are pink and firm to the touch, about 3 minutes. Finally, stir in the peas, butter, mint and lemon rind. Season to taste with salt, pepper and lemon juice.

For red wine & squid risotto, fry 1 finely chopped onion, 2 finely chopped celery sticks and 2 crushed garlic cloves in a little olive oil. Add 375 g (12 oz) risotto rice and fry for 1 minute. Pour in 250 ml (8 fl oz) red wine and bring to the boil, then reduce the heat to a simmer. Add around 1.5 litres (2½ pints) Basic Fish Stock (see page 15) over a medium heat, a ladleful at a time, stirring continuously. Allow each ladleful of stock to be absorbed before adding the next. Keep adding stock until the rice is cooked but still has a slight bite to it. Finally, stir in 50 g (2 oz) butter and 500 g (1 lb) cleaned squid (see page 12) that has been cut into rings (tentacles discarded). Cook for a further 2 minutes. Sprinkle with chopped chives and serve.

dover sole with bulgar wheat salad

Serves **4**

Preparation time **12 minutes**, plus standing

Cooking time **2 hours 5 minutes**

2 **red peppers**, cored, deseeded and sliced

16 **cherry tomatoes**, halved

2 **garlic cloves**, thinly sliced

4 tablespoons **olive oil**, plus extra for greasing

200 g (7 oz) **bulgar wheat**

2 tablespoons **lemon juice**

1 **baby gem lettuce**

10 **black kalamata olives**, pitted

2 tablespoons finely chopped **chives**

2 large **Dover soles**, filleted and pin-boned

salt and **pepper**

Cover the base of a small ovenproof dish with the red peppers and place the tomatoes on top. Season the tomatoes with salt and pepper and stud with the slices of garlic. Drizzle with about 2 tablespoons of the oil and place in a preheated oven, 150°C (300°F), Gas Mark 2, for 2 hours.

Place the bulgar wheat in a heatproof bowl and just cover with boiling water. Cover the bowl with clingfilm and leave to steam for 15 minutes. Drain the bulgar wheat, squeezing out any excess water. Add the lemon juice and some salt and pepper. Keep warm.

Break up the leaves of the baby gem lettuce and mix with the roasted red peppers, bulgar wheat, olives, chives and remaining oil. Carefully stir in the roasted tomatoes, taking care not break them up too much.

Line a baking sheet with foil. Season the Dover sole fillets and place them on the foil, flesh-side down. Cook under a preheated grill for 4–5 minutes, then turn the fish over and grill for a further 2 minutes.

Serve the fish with the warm bulgar wheat salad and a drizzle of olive oil.

For Dover sole with red pepper & tomato sauce, cook the tomatoes and peppers as above. When cooked, place them in a food processor and blend to form a smooth sauce. Stir in 1 tablespoon olive oil and a handful of basil leaves, roughly chopped. Serve with Dover sole, grilled as above, and sauté potatoes.

smoked trout & lemon pasta

Serves **4**

Preparation time **4 minutes**

Cooking time **8–10 minutes**

350 g (11½ oz) **dried farfalle pasta**

1 tablespoon **olive oil**

1 **onion**, finely chopped

500 g (1 lb) **smoked trout**

grated rind of 1 **lemon**

200 g (7 oz) **crème fraîche**

2 tablespoons chopped **dill**

salt and **pepper**

Cook the pasta according to the instructions on the packet.

Heat the oil in a frying pan, add the onion and fry until soft and translucent but not coloured. Take the pan off the heat and add the smoked trout, lemon rind, crème fraîche and chopped dill.

Drain the pasta, reserving 2 tablespoons of the cooking water. Stir the pasta and water into the sauce. Season to taste with salt and pepper and serve immediately.

For garlic & herb bread, to serve as an accompaniment, mix 2 crushed garlic cloves with 150 g (5 oz) softened butter and 2 tablespoons chopped parsley. Slice a baguette in half horizontally. Spread the butter over the bread and place in a preheated oven, 180°C (350°F), Gas Mark 4, for 10 minutes until the butter has melted and the bread is crispy.

monkfish & saffron risotto

Serves **3–4**
Preparation time **25 minutes**
Cooking time **30–35 minutes**

500 g (1 lb) **monkfish**, boned
50 g (2 oz) **butter**
1 **onion**, chopped
2 **garlic cloves**, crushed
250 g (8 oz) **risotto rice**
1 glass **dry white wine**
1 teaspoon **saffron threads**
2 teaspoons chopped **lemon thyme**, plus extra to garnish
1 litre (1¾ pints) hot **Basic Fish Stock** (see page 15)
salt and **pepper**
grated **Parmesan cheese**, to serve

Cut the monkfish into chunks and season lightly. Melt half the butter in a large saucepan and gently fry the onion until it is softened but not browned. Add the fish and cook, stirring, for 2 minutes. Remove the fish with a slotted spoon and add the garlic to the pan. Cook for 1 minute.

Sprinkle in the rice and fry gently for 1 minute. Add the wine and let it bubble until almost evaporated, then add the saffron and lemon thyme.

Add the stock over a medium heat, a ladleful at a time, stirring continuously. Allow each ladleful of stock to be absorbed before adding the next. Keep adding stock until the rice is cooked but still has a slight bite to it. This should take about 15–20 minutes.

Check the seasoning and stir in the fish. Heat through and serve immediately, scattered with grated Parmesan and chopped lemon thyme.

For roasted monkfish with saffron sauce, oil a roasting tin and add an 750 g (1½ lb) piece of oiled and seasoned boned monkfish. Roast in a preheated oven, 200°C (400°F), Gas Mark 6, for 8 minutes, or until firm to the touch. Meanwhile, heat 1 tablespoon olive oil in a pan, add ½ chopped onion and fry until soft. Add 2 crushed garlic cloves and fry for 1 minute. Pour in 125 ml (4 fl oz) white wine and add a good pinch of saffron threads. Bring to the boil and allow to evaporate completely, then add 200 ml (7 fl oz) double cream and bring back to the boil. Serve with the roasted monkfish.

spaghetti with mussels & clams

Serves **4**

Preparation time **15 minutes**

Cooking time **15 minutes**

350 g (11½ oz) **dried spaghetti**

2 tablespoons **olive oil**, plus extra for drizzling

1 small **onion**, very finely chopped

1 large **green chilli**, deseeded and finely chopped

2 **garlic cloves**, finely chopped

500 g (1 lb) **mussels**, scrubbed and debearded (see page 12)

1 kg (2 lb) **clams**, cleaned (see page 12)

175 ml (6 fl oz) **white wine**

25 g (1 oz) **butter**

2 tablespoons finely chopped **parsley**

salt and **pepper**

Cook the spaghetti according to the instructions on the packet. Drain and set aside.

Heat the oil in a saucepan. When hot, gently fry the onion until soft and translucent. Add the chilli and fry for a further minute before adding the garlic.

Increase the heat and add the mussels (first discarding any that don't shut when tapped), clams and wine. Cover the pan and steam the shellfish until they open, discarding any that don't. Strain through a sieve, reserving the liquid in a bowl.

Return the liquid to the pan, leaving a small amount in the bowl, as this may contain some grit from the shellfish. Boil the liquid for 2 minutes until it has reduced slightly. Whisk in the butter, then stir in the shellfish, spaghetti and parsley. Season well and drizzle with a little olive oil.

For breaded mussels & clams, cook 500 g (1 lb) scrubbed and debearded mussels and 500 g (1 lb) cleaned clams (see page 12) as per the recipe above. Remove the top shell of each of the mussels and clams. Mix together 250 g (8 oz) fresh breadcrumbs with 1 crushed garlic clove and 3 tablespoons chopped mixed herbs. Sprinkle the breadcrumb mix over the shellfish and place them under a preheated grill to brown. Make a garlic butter by mixing together 50 g (2 oz) softened butter with 1 crushed garlic clove. Place a small dot of butter on each of the shellfish to melt before serving.

tuna, spinach & tomato penne

Serves **4**
Preparation time **4** minutes
Cooking time **10** minutes

350 g (11½ oz) **dried penne
pasta**
2 tablespoons **olive oil**, plus
extra for drizzling
1 **onion**, finely sliced
1 **garlic clove**, crushed
500 g (1 lb) **cherry tomatoes**,
halved
pinch of **sugar** (optional)
250 g (8 oz) **baby spinach**,
washed
2 x 185 g (6½ oz) cans **tuna
steak in olive oil**, drained
salt and **pepper**

Cook the pasta according to the instructions on
the packet.

Meanwhile, heat the oil in a saucepan, add the onion
and fry gently until soft. Add the garlic and tomatoes
and fry for a further 3–4 minutes until the tomatoes
just start to break up. Season the sauce with salt and
pepper and a little sugar if it is needed.

Stir the spinach into the sauce. Gently stir in the tuna,
trying not to break it up too much, then drain and stir in
the pasta. Drizzle a little more olive oil over the dish
before serving.

For creamy penne pasta with mussels, cook
350 g (11½ oz) penne pasta according to the
instructions on the packet. Meanwhile, heat a little
oil in a pan and add 1 finely chopped garlic clove,
150 ml (¼ pint) white wine and 1.5 kg (3 lb) scrubbed
and debearded mussels (see page 12) to the pan.
Cover and cook until the mussels have opened,
discarding any that don't. Strain the mussels through
a sieve, reserving the liquid. Pour the liquid back into
a clean saucepan and add 200 ml (7 fl oz) double
cream. Simmer until it reaches a creamy consistency.
Drain the pasta. Pick the mussels from their shells and
add to the sauce along with the pasta. Season with
salt and pepper.

seafood paella

Serves **4**

Preparation time **30 minutes**

Cooking time **25 minutes**

2 tablespoons **olive oil**

1 large **onion**, finely diced

1 **garlic clove**, crushed

1 **red pepper**, cored,
   deseeded and chopped into
   5 mm (¼ inch) dice

300 g (10 oz) **paella rice**

1.5 litres (1¾ pints) hot **Basic
   Fish Stock** (see page 15)
   or **water**

pinch of **saffron threads**

2 large **tomatoes**, roughly
   chopped

300 g (10 oz) **raw peeled
   king prawns**

200 g (7 oz) **clams**, cleaned
   (see page 12)

200 g (7 oz) **mussels**,
   scrubbed and debearded
   (see page 12)

200 g (7 oz) **squid**, cleaned
   (see page 12) and cut into
   rings, tentacles discarded

150 g (5 oz) **frozen peas**,
   thawed

2 tablespoons chopped
   parsley

salt and **pepper**

Heat the oil in a large frying pan. Add the onion, garlic and red pepper to the pan and fry for a few minutes until they have started to soften, then add the rice and fry for 1 minute.

Pour enough hot stock over the rice to cover it by about 1 cm (½ inch). Add the saffron threads and stir well. Bring the rice up to the boil, then add the tomatoes and reduce the heat to a simmer. Stir well once again, then simmer for 10–12 minutes, stirring occasionally to prevent the rice catching on the bottom of the pan.

Add the prawns, clams and mussels (first discarding any that don't shut when tapped) and squid to the pan, along with a little more water or stock if the rice is too dry. Cook until the clams and mussels open (discarding any that don't), the prawns are pink and the squid turns white and loses its transparency.

Stir in the peas and parsley and cook for a few more minutes until the peas are hot, then season to taste with salt and pepper.

For scallop & pasta paella, follow the recipe as above but use 375 g (12 oz) dried orzo pasta instead of the paella rice, replace the prawns with scallops, and use only 500 ml (17 fl oz) stock, adding more only if needed.

swordfish with squash couscous

Serves **4**

Preparation time **15 minutes**, plus marinating

Cooking time **40 minutes**

1 **butternut squash**, peeled, deseeded and cut into 1.5 cm (¾ inch) cubes

4 tablespoons **olive oil**

1 tablespoon **cumin seeds**

1 teaspoon **ground coriander**

1 teaspoon **ground cumin**

1 teaspoon **paprika**

4 **swordfish steaks**, about 200 g (7 oz) each and 1.5 cm (¾ inch) thick

300 g (10 oz) **couscous**

1 tablespoon **harissa paste**

400 ml (14 fl oz) boiling **chicken** or **vegetable stock**

4 tablespoons **lemon juice**

salt and **pepper**

Place the squash on a roasting tray and drizzle with 1 tablespoon of the oil. Season with salt and pepper and sprinkle over the cumin seeds. Roast in a preheated oven, 180°C (350°F), Gas Mark 4, for 30 minutes until the squash is tender.

Meanwhile, mix together the coriander, ground cumin, paprika and 2 tablespoons of the oil. Rub the mixture over the swordfish steaks and leave in the refrigerator to marinate for 30 minutes.

Place the couscous in a heatproof bowl. Mix the harissa paste with the boiling stock and pour it over the couscous. Cover the bowl with clingfilm and leave for 5−8 minutes, then fluff the couscous up with a fork to separate the grains. Mix in the lemon juice and remaining oil and season with salt and pepper. Finally, stir in the roasted butternut squash.

Place the marinated swordfish in a very hot griddle pan and cook for 3−4 minutes on each side. Serve immediately with the warm couscous.

For tuna with herb salsa, marinate 4 x 200 g (7 oz) fresh tuna steaks in a mixture of 1 teaspoon ground coriander, 1 teaspoon ground cumin, a little crushed dried chillies, 1 crushed garlic clove and 2 tablespoons olive oil. Leave in the refrigerator to marinate for 40 minutes, then cook as the swordfish for 2−3 minutes on each side. Meanwhile, mix together 1 tablespoon each lemon juice, chopped oregano, chopped parsley and roughly chopped capers, 1 crushed garlic clove and 2 tablespoons olive oil. Season and serve with the tuna.

noodles with prawns & pak choi

Serves **4**
Preparation time **5 minutes**
Cooking time **12 minutes**

250 g (8 oz) **dried medium
    egg noodles**
3 tablespoons **vegetable oil**
2 tablespoons **sesame seeds**
2.5 cm (1 inch) piece of **fresh
    root ginger**, peeled and
    finely chopped
1 **garlic clove**, crushed
20 **raw peeled king prawns**
3 tablespoons **light soy sauce**
2 tablespoons **sweet chilli
    sauce**
2 heads of **pak choi**, leaves
    separated
4 **spring onions**, finely sliced
handful of chopped **coriander**
2 tablespoons **sesame oil**

Cook the noodles according to the instructions on the packet. Drain and set aside.

Heat a large frying pan and add 2 tablespoons of the vegetable oil. When really hot, add the noodles, flattening them down so that they cover the bottom of the pan. Cook over a high heat for 3–4 minutes until golden brown and crispy. Once they have coloured on the first side, turn the noodles over and brown on the other side as well. Stir in the sesame seeds.

Meanwhile, heat the remaining oil in a wok, add the ginger and garlic and stir-fry for 1 minute, then add the prawns and stir-fry for 2 minutes until turning pink. Add the soy sauce and sweet chilli sauce and bring to the boil, then reduce the heat and simmer for 1–2 minutes until the prawns are pink and firm. Finally, add the pak choi and stir until the leaves begin to wilt.

Place the noodles on a large plate and top with the prawns and pak choi. Sprinkle with the spring onions and coriander and drizzle with the sesame oil.

For prawn & lemon grass stir-fry, stir-fry 2 finely chopped shallots, 2 finely chopped lemon grass stalks, 1 deseeded and finely chopped red chilli, 1 crushed garlic clove and a 1.5 cm (¾ inch) piece of fresh root ginger, peeled and finely chopped, in a wok in a little vegetable oil for 2 minutes. Add 20 raw peeled king prawns and stir-fry until pink. Add 6 tablespoons light soy sauce, 2 tablespoons sesame oil and the juice of 1 lime. Finally, add 2 tablespoons roughly chopped coriander.

creamy crab & asparagus risotto

Serves **4**
Preparation time **10 minutes**
Cooking time **25–30 minutes**

4 tablespoons **olive oil**
2 **celery sticks**, finely diced
1 **onion**, finely diced
1 **garlic clove**, crushed
350 g (11½ oz) **risotto rice**
175 ml (6 fl oz) **white wine**
1.5 litres (2½ pints) **Basic Fish
  Stock** (see page 15) or
  chicken stock
25 g (1 oz) **butter**
8–10 **asparagus spears**,
  trimmed, blanched and sliced
  at an angle
400 g (13 oz) **fresh white
  crabmeat**
100 g (3½ oz) **fresh brown
  crabmeat** (optional)
1 tablespoon **lemon juice**
2 handfuls of **rocket leaves**
salt and **pepper**

Heat 2 tablespoons of the oil in a large frying pan. Add the celery and onion and fry over a medium heat until the onion has softened and become translucent. Add the garlic and fry for 1 minute, then add the rice and fry for 2 minutes, stirring to coat all the grains in the oil.

Pour the wine into the pan and leave to bubble until all the liquid has evaporated.

Add the stock over a medium heat, a ladleful at a time, stirring continuously. Allow each ladleful of stock to be absorbed before adding the next. Keep adding stock until the rice is cooked but still has a slight bite to it. This should take about 15–20 minutes.

Stir in the butter, then the asparagus and the white and brown crabmeat. Season with salt and pepper.

Mix together the remaining oil and the lemon juice and use to dress the rocket leaves. Serve the risotto in bowls, topped with the dressed rocket leaves.

For linguine with crab, chilli & rocket, mix together 375 g (12 oz) cooked, hot linguine with 3 tablespoons of the pasta cooking water. Add 1 deseeded and finely chopped large red chilli, 500 g (1 lb) fresh white crabmeat, 4 tablespoons lemon juice, 400 g (13 oz) rocket leaves and 4 tablespoons olive oil. Stir in a few torn basil leaves and season with salt and pepper.

gurnard with parsley risotto

Serves **4**

Preparation time **5 minutes**

Cooking time **25–30 minutes**

4 tablespoons **olive oil**

2 **celery sticks**, finely diced

1 **onion**, finely diced

2 **garlic cloves**, crushed

350 g (11½ oz) **risotto rice**

175ml (6 fl oz) **white wine**

1.5 litre (2½ pints) **Basic Fish Stock** (see page 15) or **chicken stoc**k

1 large bunch **parsley**, finely chopped

grated rind of 1 **lemon**, plus the juice to taste

25 g (1 oz) **butter**

4 **gurnard**, filleted and scaled

salt and **pepper**

Heat 2 tablespoons of the oil in a large saucepan. Add the celery and onion. Fry over a medium heat until the onion has softened and become translucent. Add the garlic and fry for a further minute. Add the rice and fry for 2 minutes, stirring to coat all the grains in the oil.

Pour the wine into the pan and leave to bubble until all the liquid has evaporated.

Add the stock over a medium heat, a ladleful at a time, stirring continuously. Allow each ladleful of stock to be absorbed before adding the next. Keep adding stock until the rice is cooked but still has a bite to it. This should take about 15–20 minutes. Add the lemon rind and stir in the butter. Finally, add the parsley and season with salt and pepper.

Meanwhile, heat a frying pan over a high heat and add the remaining oil. Season the fish on both sides and place it in the pan, skin-side down. Fry the fish on this side for 3 minutes or until the skin is crispy. Turn the fish over and cook for a further minute. Squeeze a little lemon juice over the fish and serve on top of the risotto.

For gnocchi with parsley pesto & gurnard, cook 375 g (12 oz) gnocchi according to the packet instructions. Place a large handful of parsley in a food processor with 50 g (2 oz) toasted walnuts and 1 garlic clove. Blend with 150 ml (¼ pint) olive oil until smooth. Add 125 g (4 oz) grated Parmesan cheese and season with salt and pepper. Stir through the gnocchi and serve with the gurnard pan-fried as above.

skate with chickpeas & olive sauce

Serves **4**
Preparation time **15 minutes**
Cooking time **8 minutes**

4 tablespoons **olive oil**
4 **skate wings**, about 250 g
(8 oz) each, skinned
3 tablespoons **plain flour**,
seasoned with salt and
pepper
200 g (7 oz) **pitted black
olives**, finely chopped
1 **red chilli**, deseeded and
finely chopped
1 tablespoon finely chopped
basil
1 tablespoon finely chopped
parsley
2 tablespoons **lemon juice**
400 g (13 oz) can **chickpeas**,
drained
125 g (4 oz) **watercress**
1 tablespoon **balsamic
vinegar**
salt and **pepper**

Heat 2 tablespoons of the oil in a frying pan. Dust
the skate wings with the seasoned flour and fry for
3 minutes or so until lightly coloured. Turn the fish over
and cook for a further 3 minutes on the other side.

Mix together the black olives, chilli, basil, parsley,
lemon juice and remaining oil. Season to taste with
salt and pepper.

Toss together the chickpeas, watercress and balsamic
vinegar in a bowl.

Serve the skate wings with a handful of the watercress
and chickpea salad and the black olive dressing.

For skate with brown butter sauce, heat
2 tablespoons olive oil in a frying pan and add
the seasoned skate wings. After 1 minute, add 50 g
(2 oz) unsalted butter to the pan. Baste the skate
wing and cook for a further 2 minutes. Turn the skate
wings over and cook for a further 2–3 minutes on the
other side. Continue spooning the butter over the fish.
When cooked, add 50 g (2 oz) drained capers to
the pan and season with salt and pepper.

braised pollock with lentils

Serves **4**
Preparation time **15 minutes**
Cooking time **50 minutes**

150 g (5 oz) **Puy lentils**

3 tablespoons **extra virgin olive oil**

1 large **onion**, finely chopped

3 **garlic cloves**, sliced

several **sprigs rosemary** or **thyme**

200 ml (7 fl oz) **Basic Fish Stock** (see page 15)

4 chunky pieces of **pollock fillet**, skinned

8 small **tomatoes**

salt and **pepper**

2 tablespoons chopped **flat leaf parsley**, to serve

Boil the lentils in plenty of water for 15 minutes. Drain.

Meanwhile, heat 1 tablespoon of the oil in a frying pan and fry the onion for 5 minutes. Stir in the garlic and fry for a further 2 minutes.

Add the lentils, rosemary or thyme, stock and a little salt and pepper to the frying pan and bring to the boil.

Pour into a shallow, ovenproof dish and arrange the fish on top. Score the tops of the tomatoes and tuck them around the fish. Drizzle with the remaining oil.

Bake, uncovered, in a preheated oven, 180°C (350°F), Gas Mark 4, for 25 minutes, or until the fish is cooked through. Serve sprinkled with the parsley.

For pollock with braised leeks, heat 1 tablespoon olive oil in a large frying pan and fry 4 chopped shallots until golden brown. Pour in 500 ml (17 fl oz) Fish Stock (see page 15) and 200 ml (7 fl oz) white wine, bring to the boil and reduce by half. Place 4 large trimmed and sliced leeks in a shallow, overproof dish and pour over the reduced fish stock. Season well with salt and pepper. Arrange the pollock on top and bake and serve as above.

main
courses

chilli & ginger red mullet parcels

Serves **4**

Preparation time **20 minutes**

Cooking time **6–8 minutes**

4 **red mullet fillets**, about
200 g (7 oz) each, pin-boned

2 large **red chillies**, deseeded
and cut into fine julienne

5 cm (2 inch) piece of **fresh
root ginger**, peeled and cut
into fine julienne

2 **spring onions**, finely sliced

2 **garlic cloves**, sliced

2 **limes**, thinly sliced

1 tablespoon **soy sauce**

1 tablespoon **sesame oil**

Take 4 squares of nonstick baking paper that are about 8 cm (3½ inches) longer than the fish fillets.

Place a red mullet fillet on top of 1 of the baking paper squares. Sprinkle with a few julienne of chilli and ginger and a few slices of spring onion, garlic and lime. Drizzle over a little soy sauce and sesame oil.

Fold 1 corner of the paper over the top of the fish, leaving you with a triangular parcel. Starting at 1 corner of the triangle, fold the edges in a couple of times to seal the fish in its own packet. Repeat with the other fish fillets. Place in a preheated oven, 180°C (350°F), Gas Mark 4, for 6–8 minutes, or until the fish is opaque and firm to the touch.

For lemon & white wine red mullet parcels, place the fish in the nonstick baking paper as above, laying on a few lemon slices, a few thyme sprigs and a little butter. Season the fish well with salt and pepper. Wrap the fish in its parcel, leaving 1 end open. Pour 1 tablespoon white wine into each parcel. Close the end of the parcels up and cook as above.

monkfish with balsamic dressing

Serves **4**
Preparation time **15 minutes**
Cooking time **20–25 minutes**

125 ml (4 fl oz) **balsamic
  vinegar**
4 **monkfish fillets**, about
  150 g (5 oz) each, pin-boned
4 teaspoons good-quality
  tapenade
8 **basil leaves**
8 **bacon rashers**, stretched
  with the back of a knife
375 g (12 oz) **green beans**,
  topped and tailed
150 g (5 oz) **frozen peas**
6 **spring onions**, finely sliced
125 g (4 oz) **feta cheese**,
  crumbled
2 tablespoons **basil oil**
salt

Pour the vinegar into a small saucepan. Bring to the boil over a medium heat, then reduce the heat and simmer for about 8–10 minutes until thick and glossy. Set aside to cool slightly, but keep warm.

Place the monkfish fillets on a chopping board and, using a sharp knife, make a deep incision about 5 cm (2 inches) long in the side of each fillet. Stuff with 1 teaspoon tapenade and 2 basil leaves. Wrap 2 bacon rashers around each fillet, sealing in the filling, and fasten with a cocktail stick.

Bring a saucepan of salted water to the boil, add the green beans and cook for 3 minutes, then add the peas and cook for a further minute. Drain and keep warm.

Heat a griddle pan over a medium heat and place the monkfish fillets in the pan. Cook for 4–5 minutes on each side until the fillets are cooked. Set aside for 1–2 minutes.

Meanwhile, toss the beans and peas with the spring onions, feta and basil oil, then arrange on serving plates. Top with a monkfish fillet and serve immediately, drizzled with the warm balsamic dressing.

For feta and sundried tomato stuffed monkfish,
make an incision into the monkfish, as above, and stuff each fillet with 2 basil leaves, 3 sundried tomatoes and 25 g (1 oz) feta cheese. Wrap in bacon and roast as above.

mackerel with sweet potatoes

Serves **2**
Preparation time **15 minutes**
Cooking time **1 hour**

375 g (12 oz) **sweet
  potatoes**, scrubbed and cut
  into 1.5 cm (¾ inch) chunks
1 **red onion**, thinly sliced
4 tablespoons **chilli oil**
several **thyme sprigs**
40 g (1½ oz) **sun-dried
  tomatoes** in oil, drained and
  thinly sliced
4 large **mackerel fillets**,
  pin-boned
100 ml (3½ fl oz) **natural
  yogurt**
1 tablespoon each chopped
  coriander and **mint**
salt and **pepper**
lemon wedges, to serve

Scatter the chunks of sweet potato in a shallow, ovenproof dish with the onion. Add the oil, thyme and a little salt and mix together.

Bake in a preheated oven, 200°C (400°F), Gas Mark 6, for 40–45 minutes, turning once or twice, until the potatoes are just tender and beginning to brown.

Stir in the tomatoes. Fold each mackerel fillet in half, skin-side out, and place on top of the potatoes. Return to the oven for a further 12–15 minutes, or until the fish is cooked through.

Meanwhile, mix together the yogurt, herbs and a little salt and pepper to make a raita. Transfer the fish and potatoes to warm plates, spoon over the raita and serve with lemon wedges.

For fried monkfish with warm sun-dried tomato dressing, wrap 2 large monkfish fillets in Parma ham. Heat a large frying pan over a medium heat with 2 tablespoons olive oil. Fry the monkfish for 6–8 minutes until golden brown and firm to the touch. Remove the fish from the pan and allow to rest. Deglaze the pan with 100 ml (3½ fl oz) white wine and the juice of 1 lemon. Stir in 5 drained and chopped sun-dried tomatoes in oil and 2 tablespoons chopped parsley. Serve the monkfish with the tomatoes dressing.

indian fish curry

Serves **4**

Preparation time **15 minutes**

Cooking time **30 minutes**

2 tablespoons **groundnut** or
vegetable oil

1 **onion**, finely chopped

1 **red chilli**, deseeded and
finely chopped

1 **garlic clove**, crushed

5 cm (2 inch) piece of **fresh
root ginger**, peeled and
finely chopped

1 tablespoon **ground cumin**

1 tablespoon **ground
coriander**

1 teaspoon **turmeric**

1 teaspoon **garam masala**

400 g (13 oz) can **chopped
tomatoes**

400 ml (14 fl oz) can **coconut
milk**

2 large **monkfish tails**, cut
into chunks

12 **raw peeled king prawns**

250 g (8 oz) **mussels**,
scrubbed and debearded
(see page 12)

small bunch of **coriander** or
parsley, roughly chopped

Heat the oil in a large frying pan, add the onion and fry gently for about 10 minutes until golden brown. Add the chilli, garlic, ginger and dried spices and fry for a further minute until fragrant.

Add the tomatoes and coconut milk to the pan. Bring to the boil, then reduce the heat and simmer for about 10 minutes until the curry sauce has thickened. Add the monkfish and prawns to the pan and cook for 3–4 minutes. Finally, add the mussels (first discarding any that don't shut when tapped) and cook for a further minute or so until they have opened, discarding any that don't.

Season and stir through the chopped herbs. Serve with basmati rice.

For garlic & black mustard seed naan breads, to serve as an accompaniment, heat a little oil in a small frying pan, add 1 tablespoon black mustard seeds and fry until they start to pop. Mix together 100 g (3½ oz) softened butter with the mustard seeds and 1 crushed garlic clove and spread this mixture over 2 large naan breads. Place the 2 buttered sides together and wrap in foil. Bake in a preheated oven, 180°C (350°F), Gas Mark 4, for 10 minutes until warmed through.

snapper with carrots & caraway

Serves **4**

Preparation time **10 minutes**

Cooking time **15 minutes**

500 g (1 lb) **carrots**, sliced

2 teaspoons **caraway seeds**

4 **snapper fillets**, about 175 g
(6 oz) each, pin-boned

2 **oranges**

bunch of **coriander**, roughly
chopped, plus extra
to garnish

4 tablespoons **olive oil**

salt and **pepper**

Heat a griddle pan over a medium heat and cook the carrots for 3 minutes on each side, adding the caraway seeds for the last 2 minutes of cooking. Transfer to a bowl and keep warm.

Cook the snapper fillets in the griddle pan for 3 minutes on each side. Meanwhile, juice 1 of the oranges and cut the other into quarters. Cook the orange quarters in the griddle pan until browned.

Add the coriander to the carrots and mix well. Season to taste with salt and pepper and stir in the oil and orange juice. Serve the cooked fish with the carrots and orange wedges. Garnish with extra coriander.

For carrot & coriander purée, to serve as an alternative accompaniment to the snapper griddled as above, roughly chop 500 g (1 lb) peeled carrots. Bring to the boil in lightly salted water and cook until really soft. Drain and whiz in a food processor with 2 tablespoons cream and a little salt and pepper. Once really smooth, stir in 1 tablespoon finely chopped coriander leaves.

fish pie with crispy potato topping

Serves **4**
Preparation time **20 minutes**
Cooking time **45 minutes**

400 g (13 oz) **smoked haddock**
450 g (14½ oz) **salmon fillet**, pin-boned and skinned
150 g (5 oz) **raw peeled prawns**
1 **onion**, halved
1 **bay leaf**
a few **peppercorns**
500 ml (17 fl oz) **milk**
100 ml (3½ fl oz) **double cream**
50 g (2 oz) **butter**
40 g (1½ oz) **plain flour**
salt and **pepper**

Topping
2 large **potatoes**, peeled
25 g (1 oz) **butter**
75 g (3 oz) **Parmesan cheese**, freshly grated

Place the haddock, salmon, prawns, onion, bay leaf and peppercorns in a large saucepan, pour over the milk and cream and bring to the boil, then remove from the heat and leave to stand for 5 minutes.

Remove the fish and prawns from the liquid and flake the fish into large pieces in a bowl. Set aside. Strain the liquid and discard the flavourings.

Melt the butter in a saucepan over a medium heat, then add the flour and stir well to combine. Cook for 2 minutes, then remove from the heat. Gradually add the strained liquid to the pan, stirring continuously. Return the pan to the heat and continue stirring until the sauce comes to the boil. Simmer for a few minutes, then season with salt and pepper. Pour the sauce into the bowl with the fish and gently stir so that the sauce coats all the fish. Pour into an ovenproof dish.

Cook the whole potatoes in lightly salted boiling water for about 10 minutes until they are almost cooked through. Remove from the water and slice into thin rounds about 3 mm (⅛ inch) thick. Arrange the potato slices on top of the fish and then dot with the butter. Sprinkle the Parmesan over the top and place in a preheated oven, 180°C (350°F), Gas Mark 4, for 25 minutes until the potatoes are golden brown.

For lemon new potatoes & peas, to serve as an accompaniment, cook 500 g (1 lb) new potatoes and 300 g (10 oz) peas, drain well and place in a bowl together. Add the finely grated rind of 1 lemon, a large knob of butter and a little salt and pepper. Toss all the ingredients together.

swordfish confit

Serves **4**

Preparation time **10 minutes**, plus chilling

Cooking time **35 minutes**

2 teaspoons chopped **thyme**

3 **garlic cloves**, crushed

½ teaspoon **sea salt**

¼ teaspoon **crushed dried chillies**

4 **swordfish steaks**, about 200 g (7 oz) each, skinned

150–200 ml (5–7 fl oz) **olive oil**

2 tablespoons **lemon juice**

4 tablespoons finely chopped **parsley**

1 tablespoon **light muscovado sugar**

1 tablespoon **vodka**

Mix together the thyme, garlic, salt and chillies and rub the mixture all over the fish steaks.

Place the fish in a single layer in a shallow, ovenproof dish into which the pieces of fish fit snugly. Pour over enough oil to just cover the fish. (If the dish is too large, line it with foil, arrange the fish and bring the foil up around the fish so that you don't use too much oil.) Cover and chill for up to 24 hours.

Bake in a preheated oven, 180°C (350°F), Gas Mark 4, for 30 minutes, or until the fish is cooked through.

Use a slotted spoon to drain the fish, and place on warm serving plates. Mix together the lemon juice, parsley, sugar and vodka with 4 tablespoons of the cooking juices in a small saucepan. Whisk well, reheating gently, and spoon over the fish to serve.

For sea bass ceviche, cut 300 g (10 oz) very fresh, skinless sea bass fillet into 1 cm (½ inch) dice. Place the fish in a non-metallic bowl with the juice of 1 lime and 1 orange. Stir well, cover and chill for 2 hours. Remove from the refrigerator, season with salt and pepper and stir in 1 finely chopped chilli and 2 tablespoons roughly chopped coriander leaves.

scallops with tomatoes & pancetta

Serves **4**

Preparation time **10 minutes**, plus cooling time

Cooking time **1½ hours**

8 small **tomatoes**, halved

2 **garlic cloves**, finely chopped

8 **basil leaves**

2 tablespoons **olive oil**

2 tablespoons **balsamic vinegar**

8 thin slices of **pancetta**

16–20 cleaned **king scallops**, corals removed (optional)

8 good-quality **canned artichoke hearts** in oil, halved

150 g (5 oz) **lamb's lettuce**, trimmed

salt and **pepper**

Arrange the tomatoes close together, cut-side up, in a roasting tin. Scatter with the garlic and basil, drizzle with 1 tablespoon of the oil and vinegar and season well with salt and pepper. Bake in a preheated oven, 220°C (425°F), Gas Mark 7, for 1½ hours.

Meanwhile, heat a griddle pan over a high heat and griddle the pancetta slices for about 2 minutes, turning once, until crisp and golden. Transfer to a plate lined with kitchen paper until needed, leaving the pan still over a high heat.

Sear the scallops for 1 minute, then turn them over and cook for 1 minute on the other side until cooked and starting to caramelize. Remove from the pan, cover with foil and leave for 2 minutes while you cook the artichoke hearts in the pan until hot and charred.

Toss the lamb's lettuce with the remaining oil and vinegar and arrange on serving plates. Top with the artichokes, tomatoes and scallops, crumble the pancetta over the top and serve immediately.

For scallop niçoise salad, season 12 large king scallops, corals removed, and pan-fry in 2 tablespoons olive oil for 1 minute. Turn over and fry for 30 seconds on the other side. In a bowl, mix together 150 g (5 oz) shop-bought marinated artichoke hearts, 50 g (2 oz) pitted black olives, 8 halved cherry tomatoes and 150 g (5 oz) lamb's lettuce. Combine 1 tablespoon balsamic vinegar and 3 tablespoons olive oil. Season with salt and pepper, then toss through the salad ingredients. Serve the salad with the scallops pan-fried as above, seasoned with a squeeze of lemon.

sea trout en croûte

Serves **4**

Preparation time **20 minutes**

Cooking time **25 minutes**

2 sheets of **ready-rolled puff pastry**, thawed if frozen

625 g (1¼ lb) piece of thick **sea trout fillet**, about 35 cm (14 inches) long, pin-boned and skinned

125 g (4 oz) **soft cream cheese**

3 tablespoons chopped **dill**

1 **egg**, lightly beaten

salt and **pepper**

Sauce

1 tablespoon **olive oil**

½ **onion**, chopped

1 **garlic clove**, crushed

175 g (6 oz) **watercress**, thick stalks removed

200 ml (7 fl oz) **double cream**

Place 1 sheet of the puff pastry on a nonstick baking sheet. Place the fish in the centre of the pastry and season with salt and pepper. Mix the cream cheese and dill together and spread it over the top of the fish.

Brush the other sheet of pastry with a little beaten egg and place it on top of the fish, egg-side down. Using the side of your hand, push the pastry down and around the fish, enclosing it in the pastry. Trim the pastry to leave a neat border, then lightly push the edges together to form a tight seal.

Score the top of the pastry gently with a knife to create a diamond pattern, then brush with a little more egg. Bake in a preheated oven, 200°C (400°F), Gas Mark 6, for 25 minutes until the pastry is golden brown.

Heat the oil in a saucepan and gently fry the onion until soft. Add the garlic and watercress and allow the latter to wilt completely. Pour the cream into the saucepan and bring to the boil. Remove the pan from the heat and carefully blend the ingredients to form a smooth sauce using a hand blender. Alternatively, pour it into a liquidizer and process until smooth. If the sauce is a little thick, add a little more cream or stock. Season with salt and pepper.

Cut the pie into slices or quarters and serve with the watercress sauce.

For smoked salmon en croûte, follow the recipe above, but replace the sea trout with 625 g (1¼ lb) cold-smoked salmon fillet and add the finely grated rind of 1 orange to the cream cheese.

sesame salmon burgers

Serves **4**
Preparation time **10 minutes**
Cooking time **8 minutes**

8 tablespoons **sesame seeds**
4 tablespoons **black sesame seeds**
4 **salmon fillets**, about 150 g (5 oz) each, pin-boned and skinned
2 tablespoons **olive oil**
1 tablespoon **toasted sesame oil**
4 **crusty sesame seed rolls**
½ **cucumber**, cut into ribbons with a vegetable peeler
1 small **red onion**, finely sliced

Spread both types of sesame seeds on a large plate, then dip in the salmon fillets so that the top side of each is evenly coated. Heat the olive oil in a shallow frying pan and fry the salmon over a medium heat for 4 minutes on each side, or until golden and cooked through. Remove the pan from the heat and drizzle the toasted sesame oil over the top.

Halve the rolls and toast under a preheated grill. Top each roll bottom with some cucumber and onion, then add a salmon fillet. Finish with the roll tops and serve immediately with extra cucumber and onion.

For sesame & coriander sashimi, take 400 g (13 oz) very fresh, skinless and pin-boned salmon fillet. Mix 1 tablespoon each black and white sesame seeds on a plate and cover another plate with finely chopped coriander. Press the salmon on the sesame seeds, then remove and place the other side on the finely chopped coriander. Using a sharp knife, cut the fillet lengthways in half, then cut 5 mm (¼ inch) slices from each piece. Serve with soy sauce.

hake on creamed spinach

Serves **4**

Preparation time **4 minutes**

Cooking time **20 minutes**

4 pieces of **hake**, about 200 g
(7 oz) each

2 tablespoons **olive oil**

2 **shallots**, finely chopped

1 **garlic clove**, crushed

50 ml (2 fl oz) **white wine**

500 g (1 lb) **baby spinach**,
washed

100 ml (3½ fl oz) **double
cream**

125 g (4 oz) **pine nuts**

salt and **pepper**

Place the hake in an ovenproof dish, drizzle with
1 tablespoon of the oil and season with salt and
pepper. Place in a preheated oven, 200°C (400°F),
Gas Mark 6, for 6–8 minutes or until the fish is firm.

Meanwhile, heat the remaining oil in a large frying pan,
add the shallots and fry gently until softened. Add the
garlic and fry for a further minute. Pour the wine into
the pan and leave to bubble until all the liquid has
evaporated.

Add the spinach to the pan in batches, allowing it to wilt
completely, then stir in the cream and season with salt
and pepper.

Toast the pine nuts lightly in a dry frying pan over a
low heat.

Place some creamed spinach in the centre of each
plate, top with a piece of fish and scatter some toasted
pine nuts over the top.

For pine nut butter, to add to the dish, mix 200 g
(7 oz) lightly toasted pine nuts with 125 g (4 oz)
softened butter. Place the butter in a piece of
clingfilm and roll into a sausage shape. Place in the
refrigerator or freezer to set. When the fish is almost
cooked, place a slice of the butter on top of each
piece of fish. Put the fish back in the oven to finish
cooking and let the butter melt. Serve with the
creamed spinach as above.

malaysian swordfish curry

Serves **4**

Preparation time **20 minutes**

Cooking time **20 minutes**

750 g (1½ lb) **swordfish steaks**, skinned, boned and cut into chunks

3 **shallots**, 2 roughly chopped and 1 thinly sliced

2 **garlic cloves**, thinly sliced

15 g (½ oz) **fresh root ginger**, peeled and chopped

¼ teaspoon **turmeric**

1 **red chilli**, deseeded and chopped

400 ml (14 fl oz) can **coconut milk**

6 **curry leaves**

2 teaspoons **palm** or **caster sugar**

3 tablespoons **vegetable oil**

1 tablespoon **coriander seeds**, crushed

2 teaspoons **cumin seeds**, crushed

2 teaspoons **fennel seeds**, crushed

15 g (½ oz) **coriander leaves**, chopped

salt and **pepper**

Season the swordfish with salt and pepper.

Put the chopped shallots in a food processor with 1 of the garlic cloves, the ginger, turmeric, chilli and 2 tablespoons of the coconut milk. Blend to a smooth paste, scraping the mixture down from the side of the bowl.

Scrape the paste into a large saucepan and add the remaining coconut milk, the curry leaves and sugar. Bring to the boil, then reduce the heat and simmer gently for 5 minutes. Add the fish and cook gently for 10 minutes.

Heat the oil in a small frying pan. Add the sliced shallot, the remaining garlic and the coriander, cumin and fennel seeds and fry gently for 3 minutes. Stir in the chopped coriander, spoon the mixture over the curry and serve.

For swordfish & tomato curry, fry 2 teaspoons each fennel seeds, cumin seeds and coriander seeds in 2 tablespoons vegetable oil for 1 minute. Add 1 finely sliced onion and fry until soft and starting to colour, then add 2 finely chopped garlic cloves and 1 tablespoon chopped fresh root ginger. Fry for 1 minute and add 2 x 400 g (13 oz) cans chopped tomatoes. Bring to the boil and add 1 teaspoon brown sugar. Stir in 750 g (1½ lb) skinless, boneless swordfish cut into 1.5 cm (¾ inch) chunks. Simmer slowly for 10 minutes until the fish is cooked, then season with salt and pepper.

sea bass with lime aïoli

Serves **4**
Preparation time **30 minutes**
Cooking time **8–10 minutes**

4 large **potatoes**, unpeeled
   and thinly sliced
4 tablespoons **olive oil**
4 **sea bass fillets**, about
   175–250 g (6–8 oz) each,
   pin-boned
salt and **pepper**

Aïoli
4–6 **garlic cloves**, crushed
2 **egg yolks**
juice and finely grated rind of
   2 **limes**
300 ml (½ pint) **extra virgin**
   olive oil

To garnish
grilled **lime slices**
snipped **chives**

Make the aïoli. Place the garlic and egg yolks in a food processor or liquidizer, add the lime juice, and blend briefly to mix. With the machine running, gradually add the extra virgin olive oil in a thin, steady stream until the mixture forms a thick cream. Turn into a bowl, stir in the lime rind and season with salt and pepper. Set aside.

Brush the potato slices well with the olive oil, sprinkle with salt and pepper and place on a grill rack. Cook under a preheated grill for 2–3 minutes on each side, or until tender and golden. Remove from the heat and keep warm.

Score the sea bass fillets and brush well with the remaining olive oil, then place them on the grill rack, skin-side down. Grill for 3–4 minutes until just cooked, turning once. Remove from the heat, garnish with grilled lime slices and snipped chives and serve with the potatoes and the aïoli.

For sea bass with chargrilled lime vinaigrette, cut a lime in half. Heat a dry frying pan until really hot and add the lime halves, cut-side down. Let the lime blacken slightly, then remove the pan from the heat, squeeze the juice into the pan and add 1 tablespoon clear honey and 3 tablespoons olive oil. Season with salt and pepper and serve with sea bass fillets, pan-fried for 3 minutes on the skin side and then 1 minute once turned over.

lemon sole with ratatouille

Serves **4**
Preparation time **8 minutes**
Cooking time **30 minutes**

12 small **waxy new potatoes**,
  scrubbed
2 tablespoons **olive oil**
1 **yellow pepper**, cored,
  deseeded and cut into 1 cm
  (½ inch) dice
2 small **courgettes**, halved
  horizontally, then cut into
  crescents
300 g (10 oz) ripe **cherry
  tomatoes**, halved
2 **spring onions**, finely
  chopped
12 **basil leaves**
4 **whole lemon sole**, gutted
50 g (2 oz) **butter**
1 **lemon**
salt and **pepper**

Cook the potatoes in salted boiling water. Drain, then rinse under cold running water to stop the cooking process and drain again.

Pour 1 tablespoon of the oil into a frying pan over a high heat, add the yellow pepper and fry for 2 minutes until slightly coloured but still crunchy. Add the courgettes and tomatoes and cook until the tomatoes start to break up. Quarter the potatoes lengthways and add to the rest of the vegetables. Finally, stir in the spring onions and basil leaves. Season to taste with salt and pepper.

Place the lemon sole on a baking sheet covered in foil. Season the fish with salt and pepper and drizzle with the remaining oil. Place under a preheated grill and cook for 5–6 minutes on each side. Dot each fish with a little butter and squeeze over some lemon juice. Serve with the warm ratatouille.

For ratatouille couscous, to serve an an alternative accompaniment to the grilled lemon sole, cook the ratatouille as above but omit the potatoes. Stir this through 300 g (10 oz) cooked couscous. Add a large handful of chopped basil leaves and a few pitted black olives.

lemon & ginger scallops

Serves **3–4**

Preparation time **10 minutes**

Cooking time **10 minutes**

15 g (½ oz) **butter**

2 tablespoons **vegetable oil**

8 cleaned **king scallops**,
corals removed (optional),
cut into thick slices

½ bunch of **spring onions**,
thinly sliced diagonally

½ teaspoon **turmeric**

3 tablespoons **lemon juice**

2 tablespoons **Chinese rice
wine** or **dry sherry**

2 pieces of **stem ginger in
syrup**, chopped

salt and **pepper**

Heat a wok until hot. Add the butter and 1 tablespoon of the oil and heat over a gentle heat until foaming. Add the sliced scallops and stir-fry for 3 minutes. Remove the wok from the heat. Using a slotted spoon, transfer the scallops to a plate and set aside.

Return the wok to a medium heat, add the remaining oil and heat until hot. Add the spring onions and turmeric and stir-fry for a few seconds. Add the lemon juice and rice wine or sherry and bring to the boil, then stir in the stem ginger.

Return the scallops and their juices to the wok and toss until heated though. Season to taste with salt and pepper and serve immediately.

For ginger, spring onions & cashew nut scallops,

fry 1 tablespoon finely chopped fresh root ginger in 1 tablespoon vegetable oil. Add 2 tablespoons oyster sauce and 1 tablespoon water, warm through and then set aside. In another frying pan heat a little vegetable oil until really hot, season 8 cleaned king scallops with salt and pepper and fry for 1 minute on each side, then stir them into the oyster sauce and add 4 sliced spring onions and 50 g (2 oz) salted cashew nuts. Serve immediately.

monkfish & sweet potato curry

Serves **4**

Preparation time **15** minutes

Cooking time **18–20** minutes

2 **lemon grass stalks**, roughly
  chopped

2 **shallots**, roughly chopped

1 large **red chilli**, deseeded

1 **garlic clove**

1.5 cm (¾ inch) piece of **fresh
  root ginger**, peeled and
  chopped

3 tablespoons **groundnut oil**

2 x 400 ml (14 fl oz) cans
  coconut milk

2 **sweet potatoes**, cut into
  1.5 cm (¾ inch) cubes

2 large **monkfish tails**, cut
  into large chunks

2 tablespoons **Thai fish
  sauce**

1 teaspoon **dark brown sugar**

1½ tablespoons **lime juice**

2 tablespoons roughly
  chopped **coriander**,
  to garnish

Place the lemon grass, shallots, chilli, garlic, ginger and oil in a food processor and blend to a smooth paste.

Heat a saucepan over a medium heat and fry the paste for 2 minutes until fragrant, then add the coconut milk. Bring to the boil and cook for 5 minutes until it reaches the consistency of cream. Add the sweet potatoes and cook until tender.

Add the monkfish when the potato has almost cooked, and simmer for a further 5 minutes, or until the fish becomes firm. Finally, add the fish sauce, sugar and lime juice. Taste and adjust the amounts of these flavourings to taste, then garnish with the coriander and serve with some Thai sticky rice.

For Thai-roasted monkfish with roasted chilli pumpkin, mix 2 tablespoons Thai red curry paste with 4 tablespoons natural yogurt. Marinate 2 monkfish tails, cut into large pieces, in this mixture in the refrigerator for at least 20 minutes, but overnight if possible. Pan-fry the pieces of fish in a little vegetable oil. Cut a 500 g (1 lb) pumpkin in half, scoop out the seeds and cut into 2.5cm (1 inch) cubes. Sprinkle with dried chilli flakes and roast in a preheated oven, 200°C (400°F), Gas Mark 6, for 15–20 minutes, turning occasionally, until tender. Serve with extra natural yogurt mixed with chopped coriander.

salmon, prawn & spinach pie

Serves **6**

Preparation time **30 minutes**

Cooking time **40–45 minutes**

675 g (1 lb 6 oz) **puff pastry**, thawed if frozen

plain flour, for dusting

25 g (1 oz) **butter**

2 **shallots**, finely chopped

grated rind of 1 **lemon**

2 tablespoons **plain flour**

300 ml (½ pint) **single cream**

½ teaspoon **grated nutmeg**

250 g (8 oz) **frozen leaf spinach**, thawed

500 g (1 lb) **salmon fillet**, pin-boned, skinned and cut into cubes

250 g (8 oz) **raw peeled prawns**

1 tablespoon chopped **tarragon**

1 **egg**, beaten

salt and **pepper**

Roll out half the pastry on a lightly floured work surface to form a 25 x 35 cm (10 x 14 inch) rectangle. Repeat with the remaining pastry. Cover with clean tea towels and leave to rest.

Melt the butter in a saucepan and gently fry the shallots and lemon rind for 3 minutes. Stir in the flour and cook for 30 seconds. Remove from the heat, stir in the cream and then heat gently, stirring continuously, for 2 minutes until thickened. Remove from the heat and season with the nutmeg, salt and pepper. Cover the surface with clingfilm and set aside to cool.

Drain the spinach well and season with a little salt and pepper. Lay 1 piece of pastry on a large baking sheet lined with baking paper and spread the spinach over the top, leaving a 2.5 cm (1 inch) border at each end and a 5 cm (2 inch) border down each side.

Stir the salmon, prawns and tarragon into the cooled cream mixture and spoon over the spinach. Brush the edges of the pastry with water and top with the other piece of pastry, pressing the edges together firmly.

Trim the pastry to neaten and then press the edges firmly together to seal. Brush with the beaten egg and pierce the top to allow the steam out.

Bake on a pre-heated baking sheet in a preheated oven, 220°C (425°F), Gas Mark 7, for 20 minutes, then reduce the temperature to 190°C (375°F), Gas Mark 5, and bake for a further 15 minutes until the pastry is risen and golden.

monkfish wrapped in parma ham

Serves **4**

Preparation time **15 minutes**

Cooking time **10–15 minutes**

2 large or 4 small **monkfish tails**

12 slices of **Parma ham**

100 ml (3½ fl oz) **white wine**

4 tablespoons **lemon juice**

500 g (1 lb) **new potatoes**, scrubbed

2 large **mint sprigs**, plus 12 **mint leaves**, finely shredded

25 g (1 oz) **butter**

300 g (10 oz) **frozen peas**, thawed

salt and **pepper**

Season the monkfish tails with pepper only and then wrap in the Parma ham. Place the wrapped tails in an ovenproof dish and roast in a preheated oven, 190°C (375°F), Gas Mark 5, for 5 minutes. Pour the wine and lemon juice over, return to the oven and cook for a further 5 minutes.

Meanwhile, cook the potatoes in lightly salted boiling water with the mint sprigs for 10 minutes, or until tender. Drain, stir in a little of the butter and season with salt and pepper.

Cook the peas in salted boiling water. Drain the peas and crush lightly with the back of a fork. Stir in the remaining butter and the mint leaves. Season with salt and pepper.

Remove the fish from the oven and cut into 4 or 2, depending on how many tails you have. Serve the roasted monkfish on top of the crushed peas and with the new potatoes. Pour over a spoonful of the cooking juices.

For minted pea & broad bean purée, to serve as an alternative accompaniment for the monkfish when served as a starter, boil 250 g (8 oz) thawed frozen peas and 250 g (8 oz) thawed frozen broad beans in boiling water for 1 minute. Drain and place in a food processor with 50 ml (2 fl oz) double cream and a small handful of picked mint leaves. Blend to a smooth purée. Season with salt and pepper.

moroccan fish tagine

Serves **4**

Preparation time **15 minutes**

Cooking time **55 minutes**

750 g (1½ lb) **firm white fish fillets**, such as cod, sea bass or monkfish, pin-boned, skinned and cut into 5 cm (2 inch) chunks

½ teaspoon **cumin seeds**

½ teaspoon **coriander seeds**

6 **cardamom pods**

4 tablespoons **olive oil**

2 small **onions**, thinly sliced

2 **garlic cloves**, crushed

¼ teaspoon **turmeric**

1 **cinnamon stick**

40 g (1½ oz) **sultanas**

25 g (1 oz) **pine nuts**, lightly toasted

150 ml (¼ pint) **Basic Fish Stock** (see page 15)

finely grated rind of 1 **lemon**, plus 1 tablespoon juice

salt and **pepper**

chopped **parsley**, to garnish

Season the fish with salt and pepper.

Use a pestle and mortar to crush the cumin and coriander seeds and cardamom pods. Discard the cardamom pods, leaving the seeds.

Heat the oil in a large, shallow frying pan and fry the onions gently for 6–8 minutes until golden. Add the garlic, crushed spices, turmeric and cinnamon and fry gently, stirring, for 2 minutes. Add the fish pieces, turning them until they are coated in the oil. Transfer the fish and onions to an ovenproof casserole dish and scatter with the sultanas and pine nuts.

Add the stock and lemon rind and juice to the frying pan and bring the mixture to the boil. Pour the mixture around the fish, then cover and bake in a preheated oven, 160°C (325°F), Gas Mark 3, for 40 minutes. Garnish with parsley before serving.

For pomegranate & coriander couscous, to serve as an accompaniment, bring 400 ml (14 fl oz) vegetable stock to the boil. Pour it over 300 g (10 oz) couscous in a heatproof bowl, cover with clingfilm and leave to steam for 5 minutes, then stir in the seeds of 1 pomegranate and 2 tablespoons roughly chopped coriander leaves. Finally, mix in 2 tablespoons olive oil and the juice of ½ lemon and season with salt and pepper.

cod rarebit

Serves **4**
Preparation time **5 minutes**
Cooking time **15 minutes**

2 tablespoons **wholegrain mustard**
3 tablespoons **beer** or **milk**
250 g (8 oz) **Cheddar cheese**, grated
2 tablespoons **olive oil**
4 pieces of **cod fillet**, about 200 g (7 oz) each, pin-boned
salt and **pepper**

Mix together the mustard, beer or milk and cheese in a small saucepan. Over a low heat, allow the cheese to melt. Stir occasionally and don't let it boil, as the cheese will curdle. Remove the pan from the heat and leave to cool and thicken.

Heat a frying pan over a high heat with the oil. Season the fish and place it into the pan, skin-side down. Cook for 4–5 minutes until the skin is crispy, then turn the fish over and cook for a further minute on the other side.

Spread the cheese mixture over the 4 pieces of cod and place under a preheated grill. Grill until golden brown.

For wholegrain mustard & cream sauce, to serve as an accompaniment to the cod pan-fried as above, in a small saucepan sweat 2 finely chopped shallots and 1 crushed garlic clove in a little olive oil. Add 100 ml (3½ fl oz) chicken stock and 200 ml (7 fl oz) double cream to the pan and bring to the boil. Stir in 1 tablespoon wholegrain mustard.

sea bream in a salt crust

Serves **4**
Preparation time **15 minutes**
Cooking time **25 minutes**

1.75 kg (3½ lb) **coarse sea salt**
1.25-1.5 kg (2½–3 lb) **sea bream**
small bunch of **herbs**, such as thyme, parsley and fennel, plus extra to garnish
1 **lemon**, sliced, plus **lemon wedges** to garnish
pepper
Aïoli (see page 178), to serve

Use foil to line a roasting tin that is large enough to hold the whole fish, and scatter the base with a thin layer of salt. Rinse the fish but don't dry it, then place it on top of the salt, diagonally if necessary. Tuck the herbs and lemon slices into the cavity and season well with pepper.

Pull the foil up around the fish so that there is a lining of salt about 1.5 cm (¾ inch) thick around the fish.

Scatter the fish with an even covering of salt about 1 cm (½ inch) thick. Drizzle or spray the salt with a little water and bake in a preheated oven, 200°C (400°F), Gas Mark 6, for 25 minutes. To check that the fish is cooked, pierce a metal skewer into the thickest area of the fish and leave for a few seconds before removing. If the skewer is very hot, the fish is cooked through.

Lift away the salt crust and peel away the skin. Serve the fish in chunky pieces and then lift away the central bone and head so that you can serve the bottom fillet. Garnish with lemon wedges and herbs and serve with Aïoli (see page 178).

For sea bream with a herb crust, beat together a large bunch of parsley and 1 tablespoon chopped rosemary with 250 g (8 oz) fresh breadcrumbs and 150 g (5 oz) softened butter. Season with salt and pepper. Spread the mixture over the skinless side of 4 large sea bream fillets and bake in a preheated oven, 180°C (350°F), Gas Mark 4, for 10 minutes. Serve with Aïoli (see page 178).

crusted trout with beurre blanc

Serves **4**
Preparation time **7 minutes**
Cooking time **18 minutes**

125 g (4 oz) **fine porridge oats**
3 tablespoons finely chopped **parsley**
1 tablespoon finely chopped **rosemary**
4 **rainbow** or **brown trout**, gutted, scaled and filleted
3 tablespoons **olive oil**
1 **shallot**, finely chopped
2 tablespoons **white wine**
1 tablespoon **white wine vinegar**
125 g (4 oz) **butter**, cubed
1 tablespoon **lemon juice**
salt and **pepper**
Lemon mayonnaise, to serve (optional – see below)

Mix together the porridge oats, parsley and rosemary with a little salt and pepper, and use this mixture to coat the trout fillets. Heat the oil in a frying pan. Fry the fish in batches for about 3 minutes on each side, or until crispy and golden brown.

Meanwhile, place the shallot, wine and vinegar in a small saucepan and bring to the boil, then leave to bubble until just 1 tablespoon of liquid is left. Remove the pan from the heat and whisk in the butter a little at a time. The residual heat in the pan will melt the butter. Once all the butter has been whisked in, add the lemon juice and season with salt and pepper. Serve immediately with the trout and Lemon Mayonnaise, if liked (see below).

For lemon mayonnaise, to serve as an accompaniment, place 1 egg yolk in a bowl with ½ teaspoon Dijon mustard. Whisk together and gradually add 250 ml (8 fl oz) light olive oil, whisking continuously. When all the oil has been added, squeeze in the juice of ½ lemon and season with salt and pepper. Whisk once again.

fish & chips

Serves **4**
Preparation time **25 minutes**
Cooking time **30 minutes**

125 g (4 oz) **self-raising flour**,
　plus extra for dusting
½ teaspoon **baking powder**
¼ teaspoon **turmeric**
200 ml (7 fl oz) **cold water**
1.5 kg (3 lb) large **potatoes**
750 g (1½ lb) piece of **cod** or
　haddock fillet, pin-boned
　and skinned
sunflower oil, for deep-frying
salt and **pepper**
crushed minted peas (see
　page 210), to serve

Mix together the flour, baking powder, turmeric and a
pinch of salt in a bowl and make a well in the centre.
Add half the measurement water to the well. Gradually
whisk the flour into the water to make a smooth batter,
then whisk in the remaining water.

Cut the potatoes into 1.5 cm (¾ inch) slices, then cut
across to make chunky chips. Put them in a bowl of
cold water.

Pat the fish dry on kitchen paper and cut into
4 portions. Season lightly and dust with extra flour.
Thoroughly drain the chips and pat them dry on
kitchen paper.

Pour the oil into a deep-fat fryer or large saucepan
to a depth of at least 7 cm (3 inches) and heat to
180–190°C (350–375°F), or until a spoonful of batter
turns golden in 30 seconds. Fry half the chips for
10 minutes, or until golden. Drain and keep warm
while you cook the remainder. Keep all the chips
warm while you fry the fish.

Dip 2 pieces of fish in the batter and lower them into
the hot oil. Fry gently for 4–5 minutes, or until crisp and
golden. Drain and keep warm while you fry the other
pieces. Serve with the chips and some crushed minted
peas (see page 210).

For tomato chutney, to serve as an accompaniment,
roughly chop 1.25 kg (2½ lb) tomatoes and finely chop
1 onion. Place in a saucepan with 150 g (5 oz) caster
sugar and 150 ml (¼ pint) malt vinegar, bring to the
boil and simmer gently for 1 hour or until sticky, stirring
frequently. Leave to cool and store in sterilized jars.

lemon & sage dover sole

Serves **4**

Preparation time **3 minutes**

Cooking time **30 minutes**

500 g (1 lb) **new potatoes**, scrubbed

a few **rosemary sprigs**

3 tablespoons **olive oil**

2 **Dover soles**, filleted and pin-boned

grated rind and juice of 1 **lemon**

50 ml (2 fl oz) **double cream**

6 **sage leaves**, finely shredded

salt and **pepper**

Cook the new potatoes in salted boiling water for 6–8 minutes until almost cooked. Drain and place in an ovenproof dish with the rosemary, drizzle with 1 tablespoon of the oil and season with salt. Roast in a preheated oven, 200°C (400°F), Gas Mark 6, for 20 minutes, or until golden brown. Turn the oven off but leave the potatoes in it to keep warm while you cook the fish.

Heat another tablespoon of the oil in a large frying pan. Season the fish with salt and pepper and place it, skin-side down, in the hot pan. Cook the fish on the skin side for 3–4 minutes, or until the skin becomes crispy. Turn the fish over and cook for a further minute. Remove the fish from the pan and keep warm while you make the dressing.

Put the lemon rind and juice, cream and sage into the pan and stir well to combine. Add a little water if the sauce becomes too thick.

Pour the sauce over the fish and serve with the roasted new potatoes.

For pan-fried Dover sole with a warm potato & fennel salad, place 500 g (1 lb) cooked, warm new potatoes in a bowl with 1 finely shredded fennel bulb. In a little oil, fry 1 tablespoon yellow mustard seeds until they begin to pop. Add these to the potatoes. Make the dressing as above, omitting the sage. Pour over the potatoes and fennel, season and serve with the Dover sole pan-fried as above.

oriental swordfish parcels

Serves **4**

Preparation time **20 minutes**

Cooking time **20 minutes**

2 tablespoons **sesame oil**,
plus extra for brushing

4 **shark** or **swordfish fillets**,
about 200 g (7 oz) each,
pin-boned and skinned

75 g (3 oz) **shiitake
mushrooms**, sliced

50 g (2 oz) **sugar snap peas**,
halved lengthways

1 **mild red chilli**, deseeded
and thinly sliced

40 g (1½ oz) **fresh root
ginger**, peeled and grated

2 **garlic cloves**, crushed

2 tablespoons **light soy sauce**

2 tablespoons **lime juice**

2 tablespoons **sweet chilli
sauce**

4 tablespoons chopped
coriander

Cut out 4 x 30 cm (12 inch) squares of nonstick baking paper and brush the centres of each with a little sesame oil. Place a piece of fish in the centre of each square. Mix together the mushrooms, sugar snap peas and chilli and pile on top of the fish.

Mix together the remaining oil, ginger and garlic and spoon over the vegetables. Bring the sides of the paper up over the fish as though wrapping a parcel. Fold the edges together and flatten gently.

Flatten the ends and fold them over to seal. Place the parcels on a baking sheet and bake in a preheated oven, 190°C (375°F), Gas Mark 5, for 20 minutes. Open 1 of the parcels and test whether the fish is cooked through. If necessary, return to the oven for a few more minutes.

Meanwhile, mix together the soy sauce, lime juice, sweet chilli sauce and coriander. Loosen the parcels and spoon the dressing over the fish before serving.

For oriental mussel parcels, divide 1 kg (2 lb) cleaned mussels (see page 12), 1 finely chopped red chilli, 2.5 cm (1 inch) piece of finely chopped fresh root ginger and 1 chopped garlic clove between 4 large squares of nonstick baking paper. Mix 125 ml (4 fl oz) coconut milk and 1 tablespoon Thai fish sauce, season and divide between the mussels; fold over the edges of the paper to seal the parcels. Bake in a preheated oven, 200°F (400°F), Gas Mark 6, for 6–8 minutes. Check 1 parcel to see if the mussels are open; if not, return to the oven for a few more minutes. Sprinkle with a little chopped coriander and serve with bread.

sea bream with fennel & vermouth

Serves **4**

Preparation time **4 minutes**

Cooking time **25 minutes**

50 g (2 oz) **butter**

3 tablespoons **olive oil**

2 **fennel bulbs**, cut into
8, herby tops reserved

3 tablespoons **dry vermouth**

4 tablespoons **water**

2 teaspoons **fennel seeds**

1 **dried red chilli**

4 **sea bream fillets**, about
200 g (7 oz) each, pin-boned

8 **sun-blushed tomatoes**,
finely chopped in a little of
their own oil

1 tablespoon **thick balsamic vinegar**

salt and **pepper**

Heat the butter and 1 tablespoon of the oil in a shallow sauté pan. Put the fennel in the pan and fry until golden brown on 1 side. Add the vermouth and measurement water, then cover and cook over a low heat or in a preheated oven, 160°C (325°F), Gas Mark 3, for 20 minutes, or until the fennel is tender. You may need to add a little more water if the pan becomes too dry.

Heat a frying pan, add the fennel seeds and chilli and fry for 1 minute until fragrant. Crush them using a pestle and mortar until the chilli has broken up and the fennel seeds are lightly crushed.

Score the skin of the fish and drizzle with a little oil. Sprinkle over the crushed fennel seeds and chilli. Season the fish with salt and pepper. Heat the remaining oil in a hot frying pan and place the fish in the pan, skin-side down. Fry the fish for about 4 minutes, or until the skin is crispy, then turn the fish over and cook for a further minute on the other side.

Place the braised fennel in the centre of the plate and top with the fish. Sprinkle over the reserved herby tops of the fennel and drizzle with a little of the sun-blushed tomatoes, vinegar and any braising juices.

For crunchy fennel salad, to serve as an alternative accompaniment, use a very sharp knife to finely slice 2 fennel bulbs and 10 radishes. Drop them into ice-cold water for 10 minutes to get really crispy, then remove and drain well. Mix together 1 deseeded and finely chopped red chilli, the juice of 1 lime and 3 tablespoons olive oil, and dress the salad. Serve with sea bream and a drizzle of thick balsamic vinegar.

chorizo-stuffed plaice & tomatoes

Serves **4**
Preparation time **20 minutes**
Cooking time **20–25 minutes**

100 g (3½ oz) **chorizo
   sausage**
50 g (2 oz) **fresh
   breadcrumbs**
2 tablespoons **sun-dried
   tomato paste**
5 tablespoons **olive oil**
2 large **plaice**, cut into 8 fillets,
   pin-boned and skinned
8 small ripe **tomatoes** or
   4 large tomatoes, halved
several **thyme sprigs**
splash of **white wine**
salt and **pepper**

Cut the chorizo into pieces and process in a food processor until it is finely chopped. Alternatively, chop it finely with a knife. Add the breadcrumbs, tomato paste and 1 tablespoon of the oil and blend until combined.

Lay the plaice fillets, skinned-side up, on the work surface. Spread each with a thin layer of the chorizo mixture and roll up, starting from the thick end.

Put the fish in a large, shallow, ovenproof dish and tuck the tomatoes and thyme around the fish. Drizzle with the remaining oil and the wine and season the fish lightly with salt and pepper.

Bake in a preheated oven, 200°C (400°F), Gas Mark 6, for 20–25 minutes, or until cooked through.

For herby plaice roll-ups with tapenade, spread 1 tablespoon black olive tapenade over 1 side of 4 skinned and pin-boned plaice fillets. Mix 1 tablespoon each chopped mint and parsley and the grated rind of 1 lemon and season with salt and pepper. Sprinkle over the tapenade. Roll up the fish, starting at the thick end, and secure with a cocktail stick. Place the rolls in an ovenproof dish and roast in a preheated oven, 180°C (350°F), Gas Mark 4, for 8 minutes.

salmon with horseradish crust

Serves **4**
Preparation time **10 minutes**
Cooking time **20 minutes**

4 **salmon fillets**, about 200 g
  (7 oz) each, skin on and
  pin-boned
4 tablespoons **mild**
  horseradish sauce
125 g (4 oz) **fresh**
  breadcrumbs
20 **asparagus spears**,
  trimmed
1 tablespoon **olive oil**
4–5 tablespoons **crème**
  fraîche
4 tablespoons **lemon juice**
1 tablespoon chopped **parsley**
salt and **pepper**

Place the salmon fillets in an ovenproof dish, skin-side down. Spread the top of each fillet with 1 tablespoon of the horseradish sauce, then sprinkle with the breadcrumbs. Place in a preheated oven, 180°C (350°F), Gas Mark 4, for 12–15 minutes until the fish is cooked and the breadcrumbs are golden brown.

Meanwhile, blanch the asparagus in salted boiling water for 2 minutes. Drain and place in a very hot griddle pan with the oil to char slightly. Season with salt and pepper.

Mix together the crème fraîche, lemon juice and parsley and season with salt and pepper.

Serve the salmon with the chargrilled asparagus and lemon crème fraîche.

For roasted salmon with horseradish sauce, season the salmon with salt and pepper and roast in the oven as above. Add a finely chopped shallot to a little olive oil in a pan and cook until softened. Remove from the heat and add 2 tablespoons horseradish sauce and 6 tablespoons crème fraîche. Season with salt and pepper. Serve with the roasted salmon.

breaded hake & crushed pea rolls

Serves **2**

Preparation time **12 minutes**

Cooking time **10–12 minutes**

125 g (4 oz) **frozen petits pois**

25 g (1 oz) **butter**

15 g (½ oz) **mint**, finely chopped

20 g (¾ oz) **fresh breadcrumbs**

finely grated rind of **1 lemon**

15 g (½ oz) **parsley**, chopped

1 **egg**, lightly beaten

2 **hake fillets**, about 125 g (4 oz) each, pin-boned

75 ml (3 fl oz) **vegetable oil**

2 large **soft, floured rolls**, halved horizontally

salt and **pepper**

tartare sauce, to serve

Cook the peas in boiling water for about 4 minutes until soft. Drain and return to the saucepan with the butter and some salt and pepper. Use a potato masher to crush the peas so that they are almost puréed. Stir in the mint and set aside.

Mix the breadcrumbs with the lemon rind, some salt and pepper and the parsley, and spread on a large plate. Pour the beaten egg into a shallow bowl and dip the hake fillets into it before placing them on the breadcrumbs. Turn the fish in the breadcrumbs, making sure the flesh is completely covered.

Heat the oil in a frying pan over a medium-high heat and add the fish to the pan. Cook for about 4 minutes, turning once, until the fish is cooked through and the breadcrumbs are golden and crispy.

Spread the crushed peas over the bases of the rolls and lay the fish on top. Top with the lids, then toast in a sandwich grill for 2–3 minutes, or according to the manufacturer's instructions, until the bread is golden and crispy. Cut each sandwich into quarters and serve immediately with tartare sauce.

For breaded hake & tangy coleslaw rolls, cook the hake as above. Meanwhile, coarsely grate 2 carrots and finely shred 100 g (3½ oz) each white and red cabbage. Place in a bowl and add the grated rind of 1 lemon, 1 teaspoon Dijon mustard, 1 tablespoon mayonnaise and 1 tablespoon crème fraîche. Season with salt and pepper and a dash of Tabasco sauce. Place the hake in toasted rolls and top with the coleslaw.

caramelized onion & anchovy tart

Serves **4**

Preparation time **25 minutes**, plus chilling

Cooking time **45 minutes**

25 g (1 oz) **butter**
2 tablespoons **olive oil**
3 large **onions**, finely sliced
2 **thyme sprigs**
2 **eggs**
100 ml (3½ fl oz) **milk**
100 ml (3½ oz) **double cream**
2 **tomatoes**, thinly sliced
8 **canned anchovy fillets**, drained
salt and **pepper**

Pastry
200 g (7 oz) **plain flour**, plus extra for dusting
85 g (3¼ oz) lightly salted **butter**, chilled and diced
1 **egg**, plus 1 **egg yolk**

Put the flour, butter, egg and egg yolk in a food processor and blend until a soft dough is formed. If the pastry will not come together, add a drop of cold water. Take the dough out of the processor and knead lightly until smooth. Place it in a freezer bag or wrap in clingfilm and chill in the refrigerator for at least 30 minutes.

Roll the pastry out on a well-floured work surface until it is about 3 mm (⅛ inch) thick and use to line a 23 cm (9 inch) fluted tart tin. Trim off the excess pastry. Chill the lined tart tin for 1 hour.

Line the tart with a piece of nonstick baking paper and cover with baking beans, then place in a preheated oven, 180°C (350°F), Gas Mark 4, for 10–12 minutes until lightly golden. Remove from the oven and take away the baking paper and beans. Place back in the oven for a further 2 minutes to dry out the base of the pastry case. Remove from the oven once more and set aside. Leave the oven on.

Meanwhile, heat the butter and oil in a frying pan, add the onions and thyme and fry over a low heat for about 20 minutes until the onions are golden brown.

Remove the thyme and spread the onions over the tart base. Beat together the eggs, milk and cream in a bowl, season with salt and pepper and pour over the onions. Cook in the oven for 10 minutes until slightly risen and starting to set. Remove from the oven and arrange the tomatoes and anchovies on top of the tart, then return it to the oven for a further 10–15 minutes until the filling has set completely. Cool for 5 minutes before serving.

crab burgers

Serves **4**
Preparation time **15 minutes**
Cooking time **20–30 minutes**

2 tablespoons **olive oil**
1 **onion**, chopped
2 **green peppers**, cored,
   deseeded and finely
   chopped
2 **garlic cloves**, crushed
½ bunch of **spring onions**,
   finely chopped
125 g (4 oz) **fresh
   breadcrumbs**
250 g (8 oz) **fresh white** and
   brown crabmeat
1 tablespoon **Worcestershire
   sauce**
½ teaspoon **cayenne pepper**
3 tablespoons chopped
   parsley
1 **egg**, beaten
sunflower oil, for shallow-
   frying
salt
iceberg lettuce, to serve
ready-made tomato relish,
   to serve (optional)

Heat the olive oil in a frying pan and gently fry the onion and green peppers for 5 minutes, or until softened. Add the garlic and spring onions and fry for a further 5 minutes. Tip into a bowl.

Add the breadcrumbs, crabmeat, Worcestershire sauce, cayenne, parsley and beaten egg and season with a little salt. Mix well with a wooden spoon, or with your hands, until the mixture is evenly combined.

Divide the mixture into 4 equal pieces and shape each into a ball. Flatten into a burger shape.

Heat a very thin layer of sunflower oil in a large frying pan. Fry the burgers (if necessary in 2 batches) for 4–5 minutes on each side until golden. Serve the burgers on a bed of lettuce, topped with tomato relish, if liked.

For crab quesadillas, brush 1 side of 2 flour tortillas with a little vegetable oil. Mix 250 g (8 oz) fresh white crabmeat with 2 tablespoons mayonnaise, season with salt and pepper, then add 1 tablespoon chopped tarragon. Mix well. Spread this over the unoiled side of the 2 flour tortillas. Slice 2 tomatoes and place on the crab mixture. Top each with another flour tortilla. Brush the top with a little oil. Heat a dry frying pan over a high heat, then fry on both sides of each quesadilla for 1 minute, or until golden. Cut each quesadilla into 6 pieces and serve with a rocket salad.

salmon with asian greens

Serves **4**
Preparation time **15 minutes**
Cooking time **25 minutes**

4 chunky **salmon steaks**,
   about 200 g (7 oz) each
vegetable oil, for oiling
1 tablespoon **tamarind paste**
2–3 tablespoons **soy sauce**
15 g (½ oz) **fresh root ginger**,
   grated
2 teaspoons **caster sugar**
2 **garlic cloves**, crushed
1 **mild green chilli**, finely
   sliced
1 teaspoon **cornflour**
250 g (8 oz) **pak choi**
8 **spring onions**, halved
   lengthways
15 g (½ oz) **coriander leaves**,
   chopped

Put the salmon steaks on an oiled roasting rack or wire rack inside a roasting tin and pour 450 ml (¾ pint) boiling water into the tin. Cover tightly with foil and cook in a preheated oven, 180°C (350°F), Gas Mark 4, for 15 minutes, or until the salmon is almost cooked through.

Meanwhile, put the tamarind in a small saucepan and blend in 175 ml (6 fl oz) water. Stir in the soy sauce, ginger, sugar, garlic and chilli and heat through gently for 5 minutes. Blend the cornflour with 1 tablespoon water and add to the pan. Heat gently, stirring, for 1–2 minutes, or until thickened.

Quarter the pak choi lengthways into wedges and arrange the pieces around the salmon on the rack with the spring onions. Re-cover and return to the oven for a further 8–10 minutes, or until the vegetables have wilted.

Stir the coriander into the sauce. Transfer the fish and greens to warm serving plates, pour over the sauce and serve.

For salmon with chilli and ginger bok choy, heat 2 tablespoons of sesame oil in a wok over a high heat and fry 1 finely chopped chilli and a 1 cm piece of finely chopped ginger. Add the leaves of 3 heads of bok choy and stir-fry for a minute or until the leaves have wilted. Stir in 2 tablespoons of soy sauce and serve with the salmon.

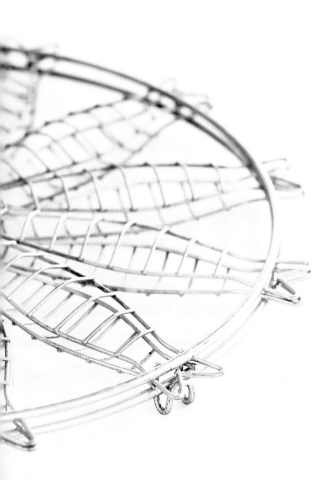

barbecue

lime & coriander sea bass

Serves **4**

Preparation time **20 minutes**, plus chilling

Cooking time **10 minutes**

150 g (5 oz) **butter**, softened

3 tablespoons chopped **coriander**, plus small bunch

1 large **red chilli**, deseeded and finely chopped

2 **limes**

4 whole **sea bass**, gutted and scaled

2 tablespoons **vegetable oil**

salt and **pepper**

Mix together the butter, chopped coriander, chilli and add the grated rind of the limes. Season with salt and pepper. Take a sheet of clingfilm and spoon the butter mixture on to it. Roll the clingfilm up to form a sausage. Twist the ends of the sausage to enclose the butter and place it in the refrigerator to set.

Take the fish and make 3 slits in the flesh on each side, making sure you don't cut all the way through it. Slice the zested limes and place a few slices of lime in the cavity of each fish, along with some coriander sprigs.

Brush the outside of the fish lightly with the oil and season both sides generously with salt and pepper.

Place the fish either directly on the rack of a medium-hot barbecue or place it in a fish grill first (this is easier). Cook the fish for 5 minutes on each side. The best way to test if the fish is cooked is by looking inside the cavity to see if the flesh has become opaque or if the fish is firm to the touch.

Slice the butter thinly into rounds and place a slice in each of the cuts you made on 1 side of the fish. Allow the butter to melt. Serve with a green salad.

For barbecued sea bass parcels, butter 4 large square pieces of foil and place a sea bass in the centre of each piece. Drizzle over a little olive oil and place a few pieces of chopped chilli and ginger and a couple of slices of lime in each parcel. Seal the parcels and place them on a medium-hot barbecue for 8–10 minutes, or until the fish turns opaque.

lemon grass prawn skewers

Serves **4**

Preparation time **10 minutes**, plus marinating

Cooking time **8 minutes**

5 **lemon grass stalks**

4 tablespoons **sweet chilli sauce**, plus extra to serve

2 tablespoons chopped **coriander**

2 tablespoons **sesame oil**

20 **raw tiger prawns**, peeled but tails left on

Take 1 of the lemon grass stalks and remove the outer leaves. Finely slice it and place it in a bowl along with the sweet chilli sauce, coriander and oil. Place the prawns in this marinade, cover and leave in the refrigerator to marinate for 1 hour or overnight.

Remove the prawns from the marinade. Take the remaining 4 lemon grass stalks and remove a few of the outer layers to give you a thin lemon grass skewer. Make a hole through each prawn at its thickest part using a metal skewer, then thread 5 of the prawns on to a lemon grass stalk. Repeat with the remaining lemon grass and prawns.

Place the prawn skewers on a barbecue and cook for 4 minutes on each side, or until the prawns have turned pink and are firm to the touch.

Serve the prawns straight from the barbecue with sweet chilli sauce for dipping.

For coriander sauce, to serve with simple barbecued prawns, place a large handful of coriander leaves in a food processor and blend with 200 g (7 oz) natural yogurt. Add 1 teaspoon mint sauce and season with salt and pepper.

piri piri swordfish with tomato salsa

Serves **4**

Preparation time **7 minutes**,
  plus marinating

Cooking time **11–16 minutes**

2 tablespoons **piri piri
  seasoning**

2 tablespoons **olive oil**

4 **swordfish steaks**, about
  200 g (7 oz) each

6 ripe **plum tomatoes**, halved

1 tablespoon finely chopped
  parsley

1 tablespoon finely chopped
  basil

1 **green chilli**, deseeded and
  finely chopped

grated rind of 1 **lemon**, plus a
  little juice

salt and **pepper**

lemon wedges, to serve

Mix the piri piri seasoning with 1 tablespoon of the oil
and rub it over the swordfish steaks. Leave in the
refrigerator to marinate for 30 minutes.

Place the tomatoes on a hot barbecue until they
blacken slightly and become soft. This should take
around 5–8 minutes. Remove, roughly chop and leave
to cool slightly. Stir in the parsley, basil, chilli and lemon
rind. Finally, add a little lemon juice and the remaining
oil and season with salt and pepper.

Place the marinated swordfish on the barbecue and
cook for 3–4 minutes on each side. Serve with the
charred tomato salsa and lemon wedges.

For barbecued pepper relish, to serve as an
alternative accompaniment, core, deseed and chop
1 red, 1 yellow and 1 orange pepper into large chunks.
Rub the peppers with a little olive oil mixed with
1 tablespoon piri piri seasoning. Place the peppers
on a hot barbecue and cook until they have blackened
slightly and become really soft, then remove, chop the
chunks into smaller pieces and mix with a little more
olive oil, a little lime juice, 1 tablespoon chopped
coriander and 1 deseeded and finely chopped red
chilli. Season with salt and pepper.

spiced mackerel fillets

Serves **4**

Preparation time **4 minutes**

Cooking time **5–6 minutes**

2 tablespoons **olive oil**

1 tablespoon **smoked paprika**

1 teaspoon **cayenne pepper**

4 **mackerel**, scaled, filleted
  and pin-boned

2 **limes**, quartered

salt and **pepper**

Mix together the oil, paprika and cayenne with a little salt and pepper. Make 3 shallow cuts in the skin of the mackerel and brush over the spiced oil.

Place the lime quarters and mackerel on a hot barbecue, skin-side down first, and cook for 4–5 minutes until the skin is crispy and the limes are charred. Turn the fish over and cook for a further minute on the other side. Serve with a rocket salad.

For mackerel with black pepper & bay, mix together 4 very finely shredded bay leaves, 1 crushed garlic clove, ½ teaspoon pepper, a pinch of salt and 4 tablespoons olive oil. Rub the marinade over and into the cavity of 4 gutted and scaled mackerel. Place them on a very hot barbecue and cook for 3–4 minutes on each side.

sardines & greek salad bruschetta

Serves **4**
Preparation time **15 minutes**
Cooking time **6–8 minutes**

8 **fresh sardines**, gutted and
  scaled
2 tablespoons **olive oil**
4 thick slices of **ciabatta
  bread**
1 **garlic clove**, peeled
salt and **pepper**

Greek salad
4 **tomatoes**, cut into 8 pieces
  each
½ **cucumber**, deseeded and
  cut into 1 cm (½ inch) chunks
10 **pitted black olives**, halved
200 g (7 oz) **feta cheese**, cut
  into 1 cm (½ inch) cubes
1 tablespoon **lemon juice**
2 tablespoons **olive oil**
10 **mint leaves**, finely
  shredded

Combine all the Greek salad ingredients and season
with pepper. Set aside while you cook the sardines.

Brush the sardines with a little of the oil and season
well with salt and pepper. Place the fish on a hot
barbecue and cook for 3–4 minutes on each side, or
until the fish is firm to the touch.

Drizzle the slices of ciabatta with the remaining oil and
place on the barbecue to toast. When they are toasted,
rub both sides with the garlic clove.

Top the ciabatta with the Greek salad and serve with
the warm barbecued sardines.

For lemon, garlic & rosemary sardines, mix together
4 tablespoons olive oil, the grated rind of 1 lemon,
1 tablespoon finely chopped rosemary, 2 thinly
sliced garlic cloves and some salt and pepper. Brush
8 gutted and scaled sardines with a little of this oil
and place on a hot barbecue for 3 minutes on each
side. Keep brushing the sardines as they cook. Serve
with a simple green salad and a little lemon juice
squeezed over.

scallops wrapped in parma ham

Serves **4**

Preparation time **15 minutes**

Cooking time **4 minutes**

6 slices of **Parma ham**

12 cleaned **king scallops**,
corals removed (optional)

4 long **rosemary sprigs**

1 tablespoon **olive oil**

green salad leaves

salt and **pepper**

Dressing

4 tablespoons **lemon juice**,
plus extra to serve

1 **garlic clove**, crushed

1 tablespoon **white wine
vinegar**

3 tablespoons **olive oil**

1 teaspoon **Dijon mustard**

Cut the slices of Parma ham in half horizontally. Wrap half a slice around the outside of each scallop.

Thread 3 of the scallops on to a metal skewer, alternating with the corals if using. Once the holes have been made in each scallop, remove the metal skewers and strip the rosemary sprigs of their leaves, leaving just a tuft at the end. Thread the scallops on to the rosemary skewers.

Season the scallops with pepper only. Drizzle the scallops with the oil and cook on a hot barbecue for 2 minutes on each side.

Place the dressing ingredients in a bowl and whisk together. Season to taste with salt and pepper. Use to dress the salad leaves and serve with the scallops, seasoned with a squeeze of lemon juice

For scallop, chorizo & red pepper skewers, thread slices of chorizo sausage and pieces of red pepper along with 2 cleaned scallops on to presoaked bamboo skewers. Season with salt and pepper, then place on a hot barbecue for 5 minutes, turning occasionally, until the chorizo is cooked.

thai red snapper with mango salsa

Serves **4**

Preparation time **20 minutes**, plus marinating

Cooking time **8 minutes**

4 **red snappers**, gutted and scaled

Curry paste

2 tablespoons **vegetable oil**

2 large **green chillies**

2 **lemon grass stalks**, roughly chopped

2.5 cm (1 inch) piece of **fresh root ginger**, peeled and chopped

1 **garlic clove**

2 **shallots**, peeled

1 teaspoon **brown sugar**

grated rind of 1 **lime**

Salsa

2 ripe **mangoes**, peeled and cut into 1 cm (½ inch) dice

1 **red chilli**, deseeded and finely chopped

½ **red onion**, finely sliced

3 tablespoons **lime juice**

2 tablespoons roughly chopped **coriander**

1 tablespoon **olive oil**

Place all the ingredients for the curry paste in a small food processor and blend to a smooth paste.

Make 3 cuts in the skin of the fish on both sides. Place the fish in a non-metallic dish and pour over the marinade, making sure it gets into the cavity of the fish as well. Leave to marinate in the refrigerator for a minimum of 1 hour, but ideally 3–4 hours.

Place the fish on a medium-hot barbecue and cook for 4 minutes on each side, or until the flesh is firm.

Mix all the salsa ingredients and serve with the warm fish straight from the barbecue.

For red mullet & basil oil, place 4 gutted and scaled red mullet on a medium-hot barbecue with a little seasoning and a touch of olive oil and cook for 3 minutes on each side, or until the flesh is firm. Place a large handful of basil, 1 garlic clove, 50 g (2 oz) pine nuts and 75 ml (3 fl oz) olive oil in a food processor and blend until smooth. Serve with the barbecued fish.

lobster tails with tarragon dressing

Serves **4**
Preparation time **4 minutes**
Cooking time **16–21 minutes**

1 teaspoon **Dijon mustard**
2 tablespoons **white wine vinegar**
6 tablespoons **olive oil**
3 tablespoons chopped **tarragon**
4 **raw lobster tails**

Place the mustard, vinegar and oil in a small bowl and whisk to combine. Stir in the tarragon and season with salt and pepper.

Place the lobster tails on a medium-hot barbecue, flesh-side down and cook for 6 minutes. Turn the tails over and spoon 1 tablespoon of dressing over the flesh of each lobster, then cook for a further 10–15 minutes, or until cooked through. This is best done with the lid of the barbecue down if you have one.

Serve the lobster tails with the remaining dressing.

For classic thousand island dressing, to serve as an accompaniment, mix together 6 tablespoons mayonnaise, 1 tablespoon tomato ketchup, ½ teaspoon Worcestershire sauce, a squeeze of lemon juice, a pinch of cayenne pepper, 1 red and 1 yellow pepper, cored, deseeded and finely diced, and 1 tablespoon finely chopped chives. Season with salt and pepper.

index

acknowledgements

Executive editor: Nicky Hill
Senior editor: Lisa John
Deputy art director: Geoff Fennell
Designer: Sue Michniewicz
Photographer: David Munns
Food stylist: Marina Filippelli
Props stylist: Liz Hippisley
Production controller: Carolin Stransky

Special photography: © Octopus Publishing Group Limited/David Munns
Other photography: © Octopus Publishing Group Limited 23, 27, 109, 225; /Stephen Conroy 6, 16, 21, 31, 35, 39, 43, 47, 53, 57, 91, 133, 159, 167, 173, 177, 191, 195, 199, 203, 207, 215, 217; /Lis Parsons 97, 211; /Gareth Sambidge 157, 163, 169; /Ian Wallace 179, 183, 187